W9-AVZ-096

ALL
NEW

DECOUPAGE

Melrose Public Library
****
DISCARDED

ALL
NEW

DECOUPAGE

deborah morbin • tracy boomer

MELROSE PUBLIC LIBRARY
MELROSE, MA

David & Charles

745,546
Morbin

19.99

5-18-04

Dedicated to Amy and Deirdre – never forgotten

Authors' acknowledgements

Little did we suspect as we worked night after night, hollow-eyed wrecks twitching on caffeine and raw nerve endings, desperately racing to finish our first book on deadline, that our crafty publisher was already planning a follow-up. No, she very sneakily waited until we were cradling the finished article in our arms and beaming like proud mothers before asking, "What about the other techniques you haven't mentioned in this book?"

No wonder she's successful! Anyway, a huge thank you once again to Wilsia Metz. Your professionalism and wonderful sense of humour (and great timing) make you so much more than just a pitiless slave-driver – you are truly a good friend.

We would particularly like to thank our husbands once again: Christopher for driving us nuts in his quest to correct our punctuation, grammar and spelling (well dun!) and, of course, we can't forget Geoff whose clandestine mission on business trips during the past year seems to have been the promotion of our first book and bringing us back interesting gift wrap. We'd also like to thank the two of you for being both Mommy and Daddy whilst we were away working on this book. The children tell us that you weren't too grumpy! A big thank you to our children: Natasha, Alexander, James and Sophie – we know that you hate to see us driving off on business trips but you all handle it well and we never come back without presents!

We couldn't have done this without the help and support of the following people: David Pickett, our wonderful, witty and wise photographer; Lindie Metz, our talented, clever and very funny book designer; Ralf Metz for feeding us when we stayed with you and Wilsia (when can we come again?); Anita Plant whose house we used for some of the photo's; Linda P for the 3D packs and good advice; Horst Stossel of Arifa Wholesale for products and technical information; Tony Mills of T M Agencies for products; Kevin O'Sullivan of Dala for his support; Veronica Lester for providing us with a room with a view in Cape Town; 34 Degrees South, Knysna, for the loan of props for our photo shoot and Bacchus and Spotty Dotty, our new canine friends (if you ever get tired of living with the Metz's there's always a basket and decoupaged bowls of food at our house).

We would also like to thank the SA Guild of Decoupeurs for making us so welcome at their convention in Durban, specifically Petro Schonken for teaching us Luminaire (which is apparently credited to Audrey Raymond in America) and our good friend June Bisschop who put us up and explained to us the difference between Elevation, 3D and Paper Tole. She also deserves a special mention for taking a late-night call when we were working against the clock and came up with a last-minute technical problem.

A DAVID & CHARLES BOOK

First published in the UK in 2004

Copyright © Metz Press 2003

Distributed in North America
by F&W Publications, Inc.
4700 East Galbraith Road
Cincinnati, OH 45236
1-800-289-0963

Deborah Morbin and Tracy Boomer have asserted their right to be identified as authors of this work in accordance with the Copyright, Designs and Patents Act, 1988.

All rights reserved. No part of this publication may be reproduced, stored in a retrieval system, or transmitted, in any form or by any means, electronic or mechanical, by photocopying, recording or otherwise, without prior permission in writing from the publisher.

A catalogue record for this book is available from the British Library.

ISBN 0 7153 1741 5

Printed in Singapore by Tien Wah Press
for David & Charles
Brunel House   Newton Abbot   Devon

Visit our website at www.davidandcharles.co.uk

David & Charles books are available from all good bookshops; alternatively you can contact our Orderline on (0)1626 334555 or write to us at FREEPOST EX2 110, David & Charles Direct, Newton Abbot, TQ12 4ZZ (no stamp required UK mainland).

The author and publisher have made every effort to ensure that all the instructions in this book are accurate and safe, and therefore cannot accept liability for any resulting injury, damage or loss to persons or property however it may arise.

Originally published in 2003 by Metz Press, 1 Cameronians Ave, Welgemoed 7530, South Africa

Publisher and editor	Wilsia Metz
Inside design and lay-out	Lindie Metz
Photography	David Pickett
Reproduction	Cape Imaging Bureau

Contents

Introduction

Welcome to the wonderful world of decoupage. Our first hands-on experience of this craft was a number of years ago when we attended a course together. Since then we have been teaching, exhibiting, selling and, best of all, experimenting.

Our first book, DECOUPAGE – A PRACTICAL STEP-BY-STEP GUIDE, covered the traditional and popular techniques needed to start and finish various projects. This was barely on the shelves when we started getting telephone calls from all over the country asking when the next book would be out. It seemed that there were a lot of you out there who were eager to move to the next level – and quickly! This posed no problem to us as we had a few more tricks up our sleeves and it also gave us an excuse to run away from our everyday commitments (again!) to try to get this new book completed. We follow the same step-by-step approach that proved to be so successful last time and, once again, you'll find a comprehensive explanation of each technique used, which means you don't have to be an experienced decoupeur before you can produce professional-looking work.

The most requested technique is three-dimensional decoupage. There are a few ways of doing this, which are explained in the relevant chapters. Hot on the heels of this is serviette decoupage which we also cover extensively.

For those of you who read the first book from cover to cover (and believe us there were many) and treat it as law, we have some good news: you can break a few rules this time. In some instances we actually encourage wrinkles in the paper and leave out base coats! In a way it's a kind of 'rebellious decoupage'. For those who want to do things properly, you will still learn to do it correctly but some finishes lend themselves to a quick-and-easy approach.

We were lucky to meet up once again with our former teacher, June Bisschop, during a visit to the Decoupage Guild's 2001 Convention in Durban, which was both fascinating and educational. All it takes is a slow walk around the exhibition hall to make you feel humbled – the quality of the work is outstanding. But most of us don't have the time to produce such beautiful works of art, which is why it's so good to learn a few short cuts. It was also comforting to hear that even the Guild members take the odd short cut or two when making items for general retail. We picked up a number of tips from several of these very talented ladies, some of which appear in this book.

We know that some 'how to' books can be really boring and have therefore tried not to get too technical wherever possible. But please remember that the steps are there for a reason. Following them will help you avoid some of the mistakes that we've made while experimenting with various new techniques and materials. Also bear in mind that there are no hard and fast rules when it comes to decoupage, so experiment, wrinkle the paper and leave out those forty coats of varnish.

LEFT *The shape of these galvanized steel containers were perfect for painted stripes. The entire container was painted white and the pink stripes added afterwards using masking tape to ensure straight lines. They were further decorated with pressed heather (see page 104).*

Getting started

This chapter covers everything you will need to get started with various projects. Don't worry, you won't have to buy it all at once and blow the household budget for the next few months! Certain pieces of equipment are necessary for most of the projects and will be used time and time again if looked after properly. If you have done decoupage before you will have a pretty good idea what these items are but, if not, simply refer to the relevant chapter in order to see what's needed.

It's always tempting to ignore sections like these introductory chapters and get stuck in to a project immediately but, if you've got this far, we encourage you to read on because we've included a number of new ideas and handy tips.

Those of you who read the first book will already have come across some of this information but do look carefully – we've added some extras.

RIGHT *This lamp was decorated using the mulberry paper and the luminaire technique (see page 72). The beauty of using this technique on a large hurricane lamp is that it doesn't only have to be used as it was intended. It doubles up as a vase for fresh flowers and even standing empty it has artistic appeal. The delicate ivy works well with the white mulberry paper without either over-powering the other.*

Source material

Various source materials are available. Many of you who have been doing decoupage will already have a collection of gift wrap stored away. In this book we have extended our source materials to include fabric, pressed flowers, newspaper, shells, iron-on transfers and serviettes.

Gift wrap

Good quality gift wrap is always easier to use. This is never more obvious than when you are using it for three-dimensional decoupage because it holds its shape better. But don't despair if you've fallen in love with a poorer quality paper: with a little more care and added sealing (or mounting onto thicker paper for paper tole) it can still be used. Plain gift wrap is another alternative to painting a background. There are so many varieties and designs of paper available that you don't normally have to look too hard to find what will suit your project. Like many decoupeurs we are addicted to gift wrap and have a vast collection of papers from which to draw when starting a new project.

Serviettes

We have now added to our gift wrap collection a fantastic array of serviettes. We used to be drawn like magnets to gift wrap stands but they definitely have competition when it comes to serviette displays. It is imperative that good quality serviettes are used as the cheaper variety tears more easily. In addition to this, sometimes the colour runs and will not be quite so intense. It's a good idea to share serviettes with a friend because you'll invariably end up having far too many, even in one pack, than you'll ever be able to use yourself. Speak to your local craft shop and suggest that they make up their own smaller packs: they're doing this at our local hardware stores in Knysna and Plettenberg Bay and the concept is proving to be very successful.

BELOW The corrugated cardboard boxes were completely covered with serviettes. The serviette technique was perfect for decorating these boxes as the serviette could be moulded over the ridges of the cardboard.

CARDS, PRINTS & 3D PACKS

Prints can be bought from picture framing shops or most craft shops. The print can be used in its original form or cut out and re-styled. Prints are particularly useful when creating a three-dimensional picture but, because multiple copies are needed, it will generally work out to be more cost-effective if you rather buy a complete 3D pack. These packs are extremely useful as they come with cutting instructions and are available from most craft shops. If your local craft shops don't have any, ask them to order some (or order them yourself from one of the suppliers listed on page 112). Some greeting cards and postcards are suitable for decoupage, so think twice before throwing them away.

PHOTOCOPIES

Hooray for the colour photocopier! It enables you to make multiple copies of the same image (which is especially useful for three-dimensional decoupage) and adjust the size to suit your project. You have the freedom to create mirror images and change colours as well.

Bear in mind that colour copies can be expensive so it makes sense to fit as many images onto one copy sheet as possible. Ask your friendly photocopy assistant for help.

MAGAZINES, NEWSPAPERS & PHOTOS

If you want to use a photograph, photocopy it first and use the copy, as the varnishes used for decoupage will react with and spoil the original photo.

Images from magazines and newspapers can be used but there's a good chance of the print on the reverse side showing through so, unless you don't mind this happening, we suggest you photocopy these as well.

ABOVE *Many commercially bought photo albums are unattractive. With very little expense you can personalize these albums. An old album was covered with a sheet of cork using white wood-glue to stick it in place. A frame for the photograph was made out of white corrugated cardboard and glued onto the cork once the picture had been inserted. On Geoff's recommendation self-adhesive gold tape was used to edge the photograph. The serviette feathers were applied afterwards using polyurethane hard varnish.*

Fabric

So you thought that you had to make a photocopy of fabric in order to use it for decoupage? You don't. In fact, fabric decoupages very well and none of the colour is lost as it would be if it was photocopied first. It's a great way to decorate a wastepaper bin to match it up with bedroom curtains or a bread bin to compliment kitchen curtains. The best type of fabric to use is pure cotton or a cotton-mix, so hang on to those scraps. You could also ask your local interior-decorating store if they could let you have their old sample books of discontinued fabrics. You're not going to use them all but one or two might be just what you're looking for.

Mulberry and handmade paper

Many types of handmade paper make very interesting backgrounds. You can even get papers with petals pressed between two layers that are so pretty that no further decoration is necessary. The mulberry paper that we use for luminaires is thin and fairly transparent in order to let the light of a candle shine through it. The thicker paper just doesn't work. You will know if you are buying the correct mulberry paper because the edges are uneven and it looks handmade. Various papers are available from select stationery and craft shops.

Pressed flowers, shells and leaves

Most of us have pressed flowers at some stage in our lives and we feel that the old way of doing it (between the pages of a heavy book) is still the best. Ferns and lavender press particularly well but virtually all flowers and leaves work. The only types to avoid are waxy, 'rubbery' ones because they seem to curl up and discolour. Remember to slip the leaves or flowers between two sheets of paper when you put them in a book otherwise you could discolour the pages.

Small shells look good, but a single larger shell can be just as effective. Don't stop there though;

BELOW A pressed lavender flower and leaves were glued onto the candles using white wood-glue. This is a very simple, yet effective way of decorating candles. The candles cannot be treated too roughly though, because the flowers are delicate.

there are many interesting objects to be found in the garden or on the beach – small pieces of driftwood, pebbles, feathers and seed pods to name but a few.

RECYCLED SOURCE MATERIAL

Stamps, sweet wrappers, wine labels and old certificates (you might want to photocopy these instead of using the originals) all work particularly well. We've found that they look best on recycled objects and papiermâché because they add to the character of the item. You may have to eat a couple of packets of sweets to get enough wrappers but who's complaining? Try to avoid foil and plastic wrappers, though, because varnish doesn't adhere well.

TRANSFERS

There are different types of transfers and you need to make sure that you are using the correct one for the job. When working on wood or ceramics, for example, you could use either home-made transfers or the ones available at most craft shops. The same type of thing can also be made up for you at a photocopy shop using waterslide paper, but don't try to iron any of these onto fabric! There are specific iron-on transfers available for use on fabric. We have never seen these for sale but then we live in a small town. We can get them made for us though at our local photocopy shop. We simply take in the image that we wish to use and it is copied onto fabric transfer paper for us. You could even take in pressed flowers and have transfers made of those.

Be very specific when asking for the transfers because of the two types.

COPYRIGHT

This is an area of concern for a number of people, especially those who want to make items to sell.

Copyright exists on numerous pictures, prints and wrapping paper designs. As mentioned in our last book, our feelings are that if you have bought a print or a sheet of gift wrap, you may use it in any way that you wish. But don't make copies of prints, gift wrap or other printed material and sell the copies. Also be careful of using certain images when making items to sell, especially famous cartoon characters. There are a number of copyright-free image books available so if you are making items for retail, rather stick to these.

ABOVE *The battered and broken tray was found in a friend's storeroom. After a lot of sanding and a bit of paint it began to look good. The shape of the tray was perfect to be used as a drinks tray, which led to the idea of recycling wine labels. The best method of removing the labels from a bottle without damaging them is by steaming them off.*

BASE MATERIALS

With all the new mediums available these days there really is no stopping you when it comes to finding something on which to decoupage. From the smallest box to an entire wall, the only thing that may limit you is your imagination. There are very few things that can give you quite as much satisfaction as transforming a plain box or a piece of old junk into a work of art.

NEW RAW WOOD

By far the most readily available source of base material, wooden blanks are a blessing for the decoupeur. They don't need much preparation and most suppliers have an excellent selection of items. Raw pine is a little more difficult to find but it is available at some outlets. We managed to find someone to make up the pine items for us and you could do the same, although the only reason for using pine instead of the more readily available wooden blanks would be to put a wash over it, thereby allowing the grain to show through.

VARNISHED NEW WOOD

If you want to work with pine (or any other wood for that matter) but cannot get hold of it in its raw state you can always buy varnished items. If it is new varnished wood it won't have layers of polish and wax over it yet so it won't be too difficult to sand down. The reason for sanding it down to the bare wood is because you will be using water-based prod-ucts and glues on it to start your project and these don't adhere to oil- or lacquer-based finishes.

OLD WOOD AND METAL

These make great base materials because they often have a lot of character. Unfortunately there is a fair amount of preparation involved before you can begin to decorate them. We have covered this preparation in the section on recycling. Raid your store room or visit junk shops; you'll be surprised at what you can find. Old suitcases, furniture, boxes, watering cans or even a metal bath can be transformed into something of beauty. We find that because of the extra work involved in preparing these items for decoupage, people seem to take a lot more care when decorating and varnishing them too, so they end up being really well done and very few decoupeurs will part with them once completed.

GALVANIZED STEEL

This has really taken off in a big way in decoupage. Many craft shops are now stocking galvanized steel items and the variety is increasing all the time. The items often have very delicate, scalloped lines and lend themselves to very 'feminine' images, such as flowers. Again, a little more preparation is required to ensure adhesion of paint and varnishes but the end result is well worth it. Bear in mind that the decoupaged items are fairly delicate (they will not

BELOW *The background of this tablecloth was sponged with yellow-ochre and white fabric paint to create a colourwash effect. Once the cloth had been heat-sealed by ironing on the reverse for 3 minutes, serviettes were cut out and applied using fabric medium. The matching images were decoupaged onto the salt and pepper pots using porcelain medium. The pots were heat-sealed when dry.*

shatter if you drop them but they will chip) and are normally used purely for decorative purposes. Don't put water directly into a galvanized steel vase; rather put a container inside the vase to hold water for flowers.

CERAMICS

Unglazed, bisque-fired ceramics are suitable for painting and decoupaging. There are many items available from selected craft shops or you

may have a potter in your area who will make them for you. These items are purely decorative. They can be used to hold dry items like nuts or pot-pourri but don't serve hot foods in them. Even fruit left over a period of time creates moisture which could eventually ruin a bowl.

The completed item can be wiped clean with a damp cloth but don't immerse it in water or put it in the dishwasher.

Porcelain

Now for something that is not only decorative, but can also be used in the manner in which it was intended. Thanks to the new serviette mediums available you can now decorate a porcelain mug and drink a cup of coffee out of it (though not at the same time). You have to use serviettes for your images because they are extremely thin and almost 'melt' into the porcelain once it has been heat-sealed. The only drawback is that the background colour should be fairly light otherwise the image 'disappears' into it.

Enamel

This can be sanded down to 'key' the surface, given a coat of steel primer followed by a coat of universal undercoat, and then painted and decorated as you wish. It will be a decorative piece that can only be used to hold dry items.

But if you would like to be able to actually use the enamel item, you can decorate it with serviettes using the same medium as you would for porcelain. Once again a lighter background is preferable to a dark one when using the serviette technique.

Glass

Various glass items can be used as a base for decoupage. The glass will have to be cleaned thoroughly before you begin working on it. Any glass items that are painted and decorated are mainly decorative. They cannot be immersed in water and the only way that you could put water into a vase is if it has been

decoupaged on the outside or if water is placed in another container inside the vase. The paint may also be scratched if you are not careful with it. But again, help is at hand: by using serviettes, porcelain medium and oven-proof glass that can be heated, you will be able to both wash and use it.

Candles and soap

Yes, you can decoupage these too! Candles that are too thin should not be decoupaged because when they burn down, the flame reaches the paper and sets it alight. For this reason it is better to decorate thicker candles that burn down in the centre rather than at the sides.

Any soap can be decoupaged, provided that it's not too 'oily'. These soaps don't have to be purely decorative, you can actually use them. The picture will eventually come off but as the soap itself will also eventually disappear, this doesn't seem to be worth worrying about.

ABOVE *The serviette medium was extended to cover the entire inside area of the placemats because the fabric is fairly thin and the medium darkened the fabric slightly. By extending the medium in this way it blended well and the colour change is not obvious. The candle was decorated with wording taken from the same serviette. Take care when working with wording – you must apply it face up to keep it legible.*

Tools & equipment

Various tools are needed in order to start and complete your decoupage project. If your head starts spinning when you look over this list, don't worry. You don't need it all at once. We have covered many different techniques in the book and not all of them use the same tools. The basics are listed first, these being the ones that are used in most of the projects.

Cutting knife

These knives are sometimes called scalpels or craft knives. Cutting knives with snap-off blades are not suitable for intricate cutting as they don't have enough flexibility. It is important to replace blades as soon as they become damaged or blunt otherwise you will tear the paper. When cutting serviettes with a craft knife, ensure that the blade is razor sharp at all times because serviettes rip easily when cut with a blunt knife.

Cutting mat

If you do most of your cutting with a craft knife it is a good idea to invest in a 'self-healing' cutting mat as this will not blunt your blades like other surfaces will. Always keep the mat free of paint, glue and varnish to ensure that it will not need to be replaced for a long time.

Scissors

The best scissors to use are good quality embroidery or manicure scissors. When cutting serviettes embroidery scissors seem to work best. Ensure that the scissors are kept solely for decoupage and they will last forever.

Rubber roller

This is useful when gluing because it helps to press out excess glue and air from underneath the paper. Don't get this confused with a sponge roller which is used for painting.

BELOW We saw this beautiful hand-made paper in a stationery shop and were adamant that it would be used somewhere in our book. A base coat of broken-white PVA was painted onto the box and pen holder before the paper was glued down using water-based polyurethane varnish. The varnish was dabbed liberally over the dry paper in order to glue it into position. Once dry, the excess paper was trimmed away and the items were finished off with another 4 coats of varnish.

The rubber rollers come in various sizes but we prefer to use the 5 cm (2 inch) one because it is easier to manoeuvre than the larger ones.

Moulding tool

A moulding tool is used for three-dimensional decoupage. It has a tiny 'spoon' on one end and a point on the other. Sometimes these are a little hard to get hold of, in which case a manicure set will do the trick.

Glue

Transparent paper glue – This glue is useful for sticking down smaller motifs, anything smaller that 20 cm (8 inches). It is inexpensive, non-toxic and easy to clean up. As this glue is fairly slow-drying it enables you to manoeuvre the cut-out if necessary.

Wallpaper glue – We use this glue when sticking down larger cut-outs or doing complete covering because it is slow drying which enables you to smooth out bubbles or reposition your picture. A little bit of glue goes a long way, so don't mix up the whole packet at once.

Once mixed it can be stored in an airtight container in the fridge for a couple of weeks. In order to mix it properly the granules should be added to the water rather than the other way around.

White wood-glue – This is stronger than the glues mentioned above and is therefore suitable for papier-mâché, repoussé, fabric, dried flowers and anything else that needs a strong glue. It can also be used to glue down paper but should be mixed with a little water first. How-

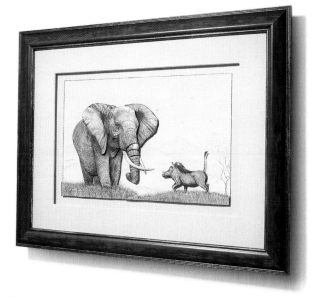

ever, it is much easier to glue paper with transparent paper glue because the white glue is more likely to cause wrinkling. This glue goes on white but will dry clear.

Clear silicon

Silicon is used as a glue for paper tole (three-dimensional) decoupage. It won't run or spread, therefore it's ideal for holding one motif on top of the other and for creating height. Ensure that you buy the correct clear silicon used specifically for paper tole (available from most craft shops).

White air-hardening modelling clay

This is used in repoussé to create height. Clay is placed underneath the cut-out before it is moulded. It dries hard and a little goes a long way. Once opened it should be stored in a plastic bag or airtight container in the fridge.

Sandpaper

Various grades of sandpaper are used for decoupage. For the projects in this book we have only

Above This was one of our first paper tole projects and our respective families thought we were awfully clever to have done it. We didn't tell them that it was really quite straightforward with the help of a 3D pack and once cut out, the 'gluing' process didn't take very long at all. It is important to use only the recommended type of silicon since any other kind may leave grease marks on your work. These marks may not show up immediately, but could develop over time.

used 300- and 400-grit sandpaper. You will need a coarser sandpaper if you are preparing old painted or varnished wood for decoupage.

Wood filler

Use wood filler to fill any cracks, recessed nails or imperfections in wood or ceramics when preparing them for decoupage. This product is water-based and easy to sand when dry.

Foam applicator and roller

These come in various sizes and are ideal to use for decoupage because they don't leave stroke marks. The best ones to use are firm, high-density foam because they last longer. The less 'dense' variety become floppy after being used a few times. Never use these applicators with any paint or varnish that needs to be cleaned up with turpentine because this ruins the applicator.

A foam or sponge roller can be used when painting larger items. This will give a slightly textured finish to the painted item.

Brushes

It is advisable to use brushes when working with any product that needs to be cleaned up with turpen-

tine (such as oil-based varnish) or when painting large surfaces. We prefer to keep our varnishing and painting brushes separate because there is nothing quite as irritating as having to pick out bits of dried paint from a newly varnished surface.

We recommend investing in good quality brushes because they are less likely to shed bristles while you're painting.

MEDIUM AND FINE ARTIST'S BRUSHES are ideal to use when painting small details and borders. The fine brushes are also used for painting over the white edges when doing three-dimensional decoupage.

FLAT, SOFT SYNTHETIC BRUSH – This is golden in colour and, because it is so soft, works very well with serviettes. It's more expensive than the average artist's brush so look after it well and try to keep it exclusively for serviette decoupage.

WHITE KITCHEN WIPES

These are used during the gluing process to protect the print when using a roller. They come in handy for cleaning away excess glue. We used to use nappy liners but the new variety is silky and, while they may well be better for a baby's bottom, they are difficult to work with for decoupage. Don't confuse these with paper towels: the wipes are the perforated, washable variety. Use only the plain white wipes as the colours in the others will run and could spoil your project.

FELT AND CORK

In order to give your decoupage a really professional finish we recom-mend gluing either cork or felt to the base. This also prevents scratches on the surface where you display your completed decoupaged item. Self-adhesive felt can be used or you can simply glue felt or cork on with white wood-glue, leave to dry and trim away any excess cork or felt afterwards.

MISCELLANEOUS ITEMS

These are not essential items, but we use them every now and again to make our lives easier, cover up mistakes and give our work a pro-fessional finish:

METAL RULER: This is handy to use when cutting long straight lines. The reason a metal ruler is prefer-able is because the blade of a craft knife tends to cut into wooden or plastic ones.

COLOURED PENCILS: They are ideal for covering decoupage's little mis-haps, like white edges or pictures that have been torn in the gluing process. Always use the pencils be-fore you put a layer of varnish over the glued-down picture otherwise they won't work. Soft, good quality pencils are best but make sure that they are not water-soluble otherwise they will run when varnish is put over them.

HB PENCIL: This pencil is soft, yet visible and ideal for marking the position in which the cut-outs are to be glued in place. Make sure you clean away any visible pencil marks before varnishing.

WATER-SOLUBLE PEN: This is used in serviette decoupage to mark the position of your cut-out. You can buy one at most fabric shops.

Varnish, resin and paint

There is a large selection of paints and varnishes available and sometimes it's worthwhile to experiment a little and find out what works best for you. It's also important to choose the right varnish for the job. Anything that has to stand up to a lot of wear and tear is going to need a strong finish.

There is one very important rule when it comes to paints and varnishes: oil-based product can be used over water-based or acrylic product but never the other way around. The reason that we always start off with water-based products is because the only glues that work well for decoupage are water-based and therefore can only be used over water-based or acrylic paints.

Modge Podge

No decoupeur can afford to be without Modge Podge. It is used to seal images before cutting them out because it hardens and protects the paper. It is also used to seal the painted item before gluing the cutouts into place. If you want to bury the images under many layers of varnish, Modge Podge is ideal because it dries quickly and sands fairly easily.

The only drawbacks with this varnish are that it is a soft varnish, it's not heat resistant and it can be a little 'sticky' when two podged items are placed on top of each other (for instance a box base and lid). One of the ways to avoid the two surfaces sticking is to rub soap on the areas where they touch or to use a coat of water-based polyurethane only on these sections.

Modge Podge has a slightly milky appearance when applied but dries clear. Be sure to apply it evenly and smoothly. Clean applicators and brushes after use with either water or soap and water.

TIP: When using Modge Podge to build up many layers in one day, wrap the applicator in a plastic bag between coats and only wash it at the end of the day. It's more cost-effective because you don't use as much varnish and it also means that you're not trying to dry wet applicators between coats.

Polyurethane varnish

There are different types of polyurethane varnish. The easiest to use is the water-based one as it's less likely to run and dries fairly quickly. It's also heat-resistant (up to a point – don't take a pot directly off the stove and place it on something sealed with this varnish) and scuff resistant. Even though it goes on white, it dries clear so it won't change the colour of your work.

This varnish also works very well with serviettes on wood and luminairies because it is thin and easy to apply and therefore doesn't damage the delicate serviette.

The varnish is available in gloss or matt and should be applied smoothly and evenly. Brushes and applicators should be cleaned after use with soap and water.

If you're making a larger item or something that may take a little more battering, try using an oil-based polyurethane varnish. It's a lot more cost effective but it does have a slightly yellowing effect on your work.

Funnily enough though, sometimes this colour change actually enhances decoupage because it can give your work a mellow, aged look. This varnish takes between four and six hours to dry, depending on the weather, and is available in gloss or matt. Brushes need to be cleaned with turpentine after use.

TIP: Any polyurethane varnish should be stirred well before use. If you're using matt varnish keep on stirring until your arm aches as the stuff that makes it matt has a tendency to sit and sulk at the bottom of the can. Insufficiently-stirred matt varnish has a tendency to look suspiciously glossy. Don't shake the bottle or can because all you do is create bubbles and problems for yourself.

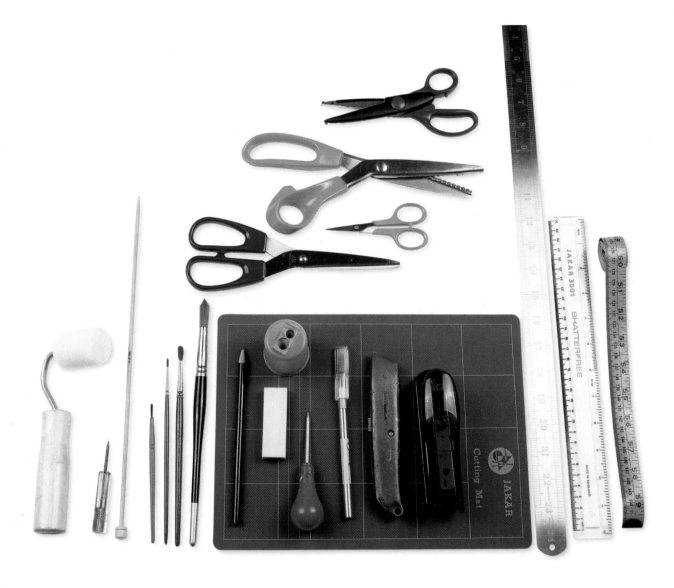

Oil-Based Varnish

These are the real tough varnishes. Unfortunately they are also the most yellow. This yellowing effect is less noticeable on a dark background and, as mentioned before, can give an aged look to an item. Bear in mind that the more coats you apply, the more yellow your item becomes and over time it will become yellower still.

Try to use a fairly thin varnish because the thicker it is, the more difficult it is to apply. Shake the can before buying it: if it sounds like cream then it's just right. Avoid the ones that are too thick.

Oil-based varnish usually takes about 24 hours to dry but do check the tin for exact drying times. The surface will often feel dry but just underneath the surface the varnish is still tacky. A second coat applied at this point can result in some very weird reactions. If you are using multiple layers of an oil-based varnish bear in mind that your item can take up to a month to 'cure'

BELOW We used left-over scraps of material from a child's duvet set to cover the CD box and cylinder which is used to store anything from pencils to hair accessories. The fabric also serves to strengthen the cardboard cylinder which has taken a lot of battering but still looks good.

properly, depending on the weather. Oil-based varnishes are usually available in gloss or matt. Brushes should be cleaned with turpentine.

TIP: Be careful of runs! These can occur very easily, especially on corners. If you do have runs, carefully scrape them away with a craft knife and apply another coat of varnish.

RESIN

Resin is a high-gloss polymer coating which is perfect for burying images in a single pouring. It can be a little tricky for first-time users because you have to mix equal amounts of two products together before using it. Once mixed, the resin must be used immediately otherwise it starts to thicken and becomes difficult to work with. When working with resin keep the cat away from your work because hair, fluff and dust are your biggest enemy.

You don't use brushes or applicators when working with resin – it's manipulated with an ice cream stick. Be sure to work on a flat surface because this product is self levelling and if your surface is uneven, your resin will be too. Sometimes a 'double-pouring' is necessary to bury thicker objects such as shells. Unfortunately resin will also yellow over time and even quicker if applied thickly. This is hardly noticeable on a dark background but very obvious on a light one. It takes about 48 hours to dry and then a further two week's curing time.

TIP: If you have hairs or fluff in the dry resin, sand with 300-grit sandpaper, re-mix and re-pour.

PORCELAIN MEDIUM

This medium is used over serviettes in order to 'glue' them in place. It's a water-based product that can be used on enamel, porcelain and glass. Don't be put off by the small bottles (though larger sizes are available) as a little goes a long way. Porcelain medium is available at most good craft shops. Wash brushes with soap and water.

TIP: Surfaces must be dust- and grease-free before using this medium. Wipe with methylated spirits.

TEXTILE MEDIUM

This product is also used over serviettes. It is also water-based and can be used on cotton and cotton-mix fabrics. It comes in small and large quantities but you need to use twice as much textile medium as porcelain medium. So if your project is a fairly large one it's best to buy the bigger size. Brushes need to be washed with soap and water.

TIP: Fabric should be washed first to remove any sizing or proofing.

LACQUER MEDIUM

This is also for use over serviettes. Again, it's water-based (which is unique in a lacquer) and can be used on wood, metal, tin, ceramics, cardboard, candles, soap and plastic. The medium comes in gloss, matt or silk matt. Brushes can be washed in soap and water.

TIP: Surfaces should be clean and dust-free before using this medium.

CANDLE MEDIUM

This medium is used on soap and (you guessed it!) candles. It's a water-based product and can be used to 'glue' either serviette or paper cut-outs in place. One drawback to this product is a tendency towards stickiness even after drying and we suggest that you put a layer of water-based polyurethane over it to overcome this problem. Brushes should be cleaned with soapy water.

TIP: This medium can be mixed in equal parts with paint and used to paint the candle before decorating.

Poster and water-colour varnish

Two coats of this varnish which we only use for paper tole (three-dimensional decoupage) give your work a porcelain-like appearance. It is available from good art supply and stationery shops. It is applied through a fabric painting bottle with a nozzle so no brushes are needed. Any spills and messes can be cleaned up with acetone (but please remember that acetone melts varnish, false nails and so on!).

TIP: Don't sniff this stuff: it'll make you dizzy!

Scumble glaze

This isn't a varnish nor a paint in the strict sense of the word but we needed to slot it in somewhere and here seems as good a spot as any. It's used in combination with paint and water in order to keep the paint 'workable' for longer. We use it when applying colour washes to wood or when antiquing. Be sure to buy an acrylic scumble glaze to use in conjunction with acrylic or water-based paints. Brushes can be washed in soapy water.

TIP: The general mix for antiquing is 1 part raw umber artist's acrylic paint, 2 parts scumble glaze and 3 parts water.

Paints

As mentioned earlier in this section, we always use water-based paints. These paints include PVA and acrylics. If you're not sure, read the bottle or tin: if it says it can be diluted or cleaned up with water then it's water-based. Ever since we started doing decoupage we have always had a tin of broken-white PVA around. It's ideal for base coats and it's also a good base colour for washes and antiquing.

There are literally hundreds of different colours of acrylic craft paints available and they come in small sizes so you don't end up wasting money or paint. These little bottles are available at craft shops and many hardware stores. Obviously, if your project is a fairly large one it would be more cost-effective to buy a bigger tin.

Remember, when buying tins of paint, check the colour charts as virtually any colour can be mixed for you. While you can use acrylics, it's best not to buy one of the special 'super-washable' paints that can be used on exterior walls: they have so much acrylic in them that sanding becomes difficult.

It's best to use foam applicators for applying paint, unless you are working on a large project, in which case a paintbrush or foam roller is better. Applicators, rollers and brushes can be cleaned with soap and water.

TIP: Paint that dries quickly can be a real pain to work with: you can never get a smooth finish because it starts to dry as soon as you put it on and then forces you to work too quickly. If you're battling with this problem you can add acrylic paint extender or change your brand – there are many from which to choose.

WATERCOLOUR SET

We use watercolours to touch up the white edges of our three-dimensional decoupage. An expensive set isn't necessary: we use our children's paints. For those of you who can't remember how to use them because it's been too long since grade school and your kids have left home, it's really easy. Wet your brush, brush it over the colour of your choice a few times and that's it – you have paint. Wash brushes with water.

TIP: Don't stick the brush in your eye! (Working with watercolours is so simple that this is the only tip we could think of.)

BELOW As this box was sanded to give it an aged effect, we omitted the scumble glaze when applying the wash (1 part water, 1 part paint) because paint is easier to sand without it. Another option to give an even more aged effect would be to antique the wash after it has been sanded.

Preparation

We all know that this can be boring but it is necessary. There have been many times when we were raring to go on a new project and wanted to wave a magic wand to take us past the preparation stage. We even tried to convince our husbands that applying base coats and filling in holes with wood filler is really quite exciting to get them to do it but, unfortunately, they're not as daft as they look. The good news is that for many techniques in this book preparation is minimal and, in some cases, it's virtually non-existent. Having said that though, it's important that where a little more preparation is called for, it should be done properly to ensure a good end result.

Preparation covers everything from planning and visualising the end result right through to gluing. Owing to the fact that this book has so many diverse techniques, a lot of the preparation falls into the specific sections. In this section we will go through the basic preparation for wood, ceramics and galvanized steel because a lot of the techniques explained can be applied to these surfaces. We will also go through basic cutting and gluing techniques although, once again, there are further notes in the relevant chapters.

LEFT *A cut-to-size piece of paper was used to cover the inside of the tray while a single image was cut out for the serviette holder. The edges of the pine tray and serviette holder were colourwashed using a white mix and sealed with a polyurethane varnish. The tray was completed with resin which is hard-wearing and gives a beautiful high-gloss finish.*

PREPARING BASE MATERIALS

BELOW The chest and the lamp base were painted with broken-white PVA and then antiqued with a traditional raw-umber mix. There was still something missing so we applied a yellow ochre and cadmium-yellow glaze over the antiquing to give it an 'olde worlde' look. The same aged, yellow effect could be achieved by finishing the item off with 2-3 coats of oil-based varnish.

In order to give your decoupage a professional finish, it needs a professional start. It's no good putting a lot of time and effort into something that feels rough to the touch and has visible holes or imperfections. Holes or imperfections are only attractive when they are there intentionally (an old wooden box or a battered watering can for instance). Rough wood is never a bonus though. It's difficult to glue onto and, even if you do manage to get the gluing right, it eventually becomes a dust collector that is difficult to clean. An important aspect about decoupage is that people seem to love running their hands over it and a rough, non-sanded surface just doesn't feel right.

Ceramics

These are bisque-fired, blank ceramics that are usually sold for ceramic painting. If you can't find them in your area, a local potter should be able to make them up for you. Another option is to use unglazed clay flowerpots and these are available at most nurseries. Dried flowers and repoussé work well on ceramics but remember that you'll probably be working on a curved surface so, if you are still a novice, start with something small.

Bear in mind that the items you produce are purely for decorative purposes. Bowls or jars can be used to store dry ingredients because they can simply be wiped clean. Decoupaged ceramics should not be submerged in water as this will eventually destroy the finish.

The preparation for ceramics is exactly the same as for new wood. Bisque ceramics are easily broken before being decoupaged so they need to be handled with care.

Galvanized steel

When preparing to decoupage onto galvanized steel you can throw away the sandpaper and filler. The odd dent adds to the appeal of these items and sanding is unnecessary. As mentioned before these items are purely decorative and should not be used to store water. Once again repoussé and dried flowers work well on this surface.

In order to prepare the surface for decoupage the following steps are necessary:

- Thoroughly clean the galvanized steel with galvanized iron-cleaner (as explained in the manufacturer's instructions) from your local hardware store. Use a stiff metal brush or scouring pad.
- Apply a thick coat of galvanized steel metal-primer. Leave to dry.
- If you have managed to get hold of one of the new primers that don't require an undercoat you can now begin painting the surface with the acrylic colour of your choice. But if the instructions state that an undercoat is required, apply this before painting the item with acrylic paint.

Wood

When using wood in our classes and demonstrations we are often asked why a base coat should be applied before sanding and not the other way around. The reason for this is that water-based products lift the fibres of the wood when first applied so it makes sense to start sanding only once the fibres have been lifted.

The first coat of paint also serves to highlight imperfections such as gaps or holes which are not always noticeable when the wood is in its raw state.

When working on new wood, follow these steps unless otherwise stipulated in the relevant chapters. If you want to decoupage onto old wood refer to the section on recycling (page 88) to find out how to get rid of old paint and varnish before continuing with these steps.

YOU WILL NEED
Broken white PVA paint
Foam applicator
Wood filler
400-grit sandpaper
Acrylic paint in colour of choice
Modge Podge

1 Apply a base coat of broken-white PVA to the entire surface of the item, inside and out. Leave to dry.

2 Fill all blemishes, recessed nails and holes with wood filler. Try to apply the filler as smoothly as possible in order to make sanding easier. Leave to dry.

3 Dry-sand the entire item with 400-grit sandpaper. Make sure there are no rough edges and that the wood filler is smooth.

4 Paint the inside and outside of the item with the colour of your choice allowing drying time between coats. Three to four coats are required for a good coverage.

5 When dry, apply a coat of Modge Podge over the entire item to protect the painted surface for gluing.

Cutting techniques

For those of you who don't know it already, the word 'decoupage' comes from the French word, 'couper', which means, 'to cut'. Cutting is therefore one of the most important aspects of this craft. There have been many times when we have come across decoupaged items where bad cutting has ruined what would have been an otherwise good finish.

If you are working with serviettes, the following techniques do not apply; refer to the relevant section where cutting and sealing of serviettes are explained (see page 41).

It is important to seal the paper or prints with one coat of Modge Podge before beginning to cut. This strengthens the paper and helps to prevent discolouration when using other varnishes or resin later on in the project. The paper must be completely dry before you start cutting. Use scissors to roughly cut away the section with the image you wish to use, rather than battling to work with a full sheet of gift wrap.

When cutting out an image, always cut away the inside pieces of background first and then move on to the outer edges. It makes cutting a lot easier. We suggest that the inside pieces are cut with a craft knife and then you can switch to a pair of scissors if you wish.

Using a craft knife

Ensure that the blade you are using is sharp and always cut on a self-healing cutting mat. If the paper begins to tear or wrinkle it means that either the blade is blunt or you're not applying enough pressure to the knife. Cut either on or just inside the edge of the picture to avoid leaving any background on the cut out image. Make sure that all corners are cut properly before lifting the cut-out from the paper or it might rip.

Using a pair of scissors

The important thing to remember about cutting with scissors is to 'feed' the paper into the blade. The hand that holds the scissors should be kept still and relaxed – only the fingers working the blades should move. The whole idea of this is to avoid 'snipping away' at the paper, which will leave a lot of jagged edges.

BELOW *We used a large enamel bowl as the mould for this papier-mâché project. A lot of patience and even more mess were involved in the making of this bowl. Extra layers of newspaper were needed, as the bowl is so big. It was painted with broken-white PVA and lightly antiqued with raw umber before the images were glued into place. The inside and delicate areas of the images were cut with a craft knife. We then used an embroidery scissors to cut the rest of the fruit.*

HANDY HINTS

- Be creative – should the image you want to use be too large for the item to be decoupaged, cut it down and resize it by leaving out parts of the design or reduce it on a photocopier. If the image is too small you can add extra pieces to the design.
- When cutting intricate designs leave thin sections of paper uncut (like bridges) between, for example, a stem and a leaf, in order to prevent the intricate bits from tearing off. Just before gluing your motif you can cut away the bridges.
- Don't worry if you have a slip of the blade and cut off part of the picture – it's not a disaster since you can simply glue it together again later.
- Cut away any sections of pictures that you would have overlapped to avoid having to use additional layers of varnish to bury them once you've glued them into position. Lay out the design before cutting away sections.

ABOVE *This ivy was crying out for a crisp background to bring it to life. The cutting is every intricate and is best done in sections which are later joined together on the cloth. We found it easier to have an original, complete serviette on hand when putting together the bits so that we could figure out which bits went where!*

ARRANGING AND GLUING

This is probably one of the most enjoyable and creative parts of decoupage. The preparation and painting is done and it's time to have some fun. There have been times when we've changed our minds at the last minute and decided to use completely different images to the ones originally intended, so don't be surprised if this happens to you. Simply put the original cut-outs into a plastic folder and use them at a later stage. If this is all new to you, bear in mind that gluing down small images is a lot easier than working with large ones, so try something simple to start off with.

ARRANGING

A little bit of thought needs to go into the arrangement of cut-outs. Now and then it will be easy and look right first time but this doesn't usually happen, especially when you are working with a lot of motifs. Occasionally it will seem that nothing looks right and it's best to put your decoupage aside and do something else for a while. It sometimes helps to get a second opinion (we occasionally ask our husbands just for a laugh, especially since Geoff always seems to think that the only thing missing is a lot of gold!).

It's very easy to fall into the trap of 'over-decorating' so try to remember the saying, 'less is more' (unless you are making a Victorian-style screen for instance, when the saying would change to 'more is still not enough'!).

On vertical sides, it helps to use a little blue tac or Prestik to hold the motifs in position, so that you can get an idea of what the overall design is going to look like. This is not recommended when using serviettes because they are too flimsy and the Prestik will damage them.

BELOW Yellow-ochre and dark-brown fabric paint were used to paint a background on the bag and apron. This is a good example of how the same images arranged differently, can work together.

Gluing

Before gluing, take one final look at your arrangement and make sure that you are happy with it. You will glue one motif at a time and, before doing this, it's best to mark their positions on the surface using a faint pencil marking.

1 Lay your cut-out, picture-side down, onto a damp kitchen wipe. This prevents the motif from getting stuck to the surface underneath. Using your fingers, apply glue directly (and liberally) to the entire back surface of the cut-out.

2 Gently place the picture in position. Cover it with a new damp kitchen wipe to protect it. Glue the image down using a rubber roller, working from the centre outwards, ensuring that all wrinkles and air bubbles are smoothed out. Never stick down the sides first because air or glue bubbles will form in the middle.

HANDY HINTS

- When gluing on a curved surface, it's better to use your fingers instead of a roller. You could also try 'relaxing' the paper in water first (this is fully explained in the section on recycling – see page 88).
- After applying glue to an intricate cut-out, don't try lifting it off the kitchen wipe; lift the whole kitchen wipe with the cut-out and press it into position.
- If you do have any air or glue bubbles in your work, make a tiny slit in the middle of the bubble and gently press down to release the air.
- If you damage a cut-out slightly while gluing, allow to dry, then touch up with a coloured pencil.

3 Clean away any excess glue with a mild vinegar solution (a teaspoon of vinegar to a cup of water). Ensure that all edges are glued down firmly, re-gluing where necessary. Leave to dry and seal with a coat of Modge Podge.

BELOW Fruit can sometimes be difficult to place and it took us a while to achieve the look we wanted on this papier mache bowl. We often find that when arranging fruit on a bowl, it is better to use more images, rather than less.

New techniques

There are so many beautiful serviettes around and it is really wonderful to be able to use them for decoupage. Before serviette medium became available, it was possible to apply serviettes to limited surfaces by using Podge. The results were never very professional, though, which is why we never pursued it when writing our first book.

Now you can decoupage virtually any surface with serviettes, with the added benefit of actually being able to use the item instead of having yet another decorative piece gathering dust on your dining-room table! We've had time to experiment with the products, iron out any problems and to find the easiest way to use each product.

Three-dimensional decoupage has been around for a long time and is a natural progression from traditional decoupage. One of its forms, paper tole, is not as practical as other forms of decoupage because you are basically restricted to making pictures and cards. It can be applied to other surfaces, but is delicate and with handling will become damaged over time. But, it is really satisfying to complete one of these pictures (and everyone thinks you are brilliant when you do) so go ahead and make at least one.

If you like the idea of three-dimensional decoupage but would like to make something more practical, repoussé is the answer. The images are built up with clay in order to create height, texture and detail. This form of three-dimensional decoupage can be as detailed or as simple as you wish to make it.

Using decoupage in various forms to recycle old junk is our contribution to the environment. In addition we've used natural objects such as pressed flowers and leaves, feathers and shells to decorate everyday items, thus bringing nature into the home.

We show you how to decoupage with, as well as onto, fabric (including iron-on transfers, even though this is not decoupage in the strict sense of the word), and how to create exquisite gifts costing you little more than time with a combination of papier-mâché and decoupage. Also included are luminaires with mulberry or rice paper, fast becoming one of the most popular decoupage techniques.

These, together with serviette and three-dimensional decoupage, have become the 'new decoupage'. We have had numerous requests from both beginners and others who want to move on to the next stage.

Some of the methods we explain are so simple you'll be amazed at how quickly your project is finished. Others, like three-dimensional decoupage, take longer, but you will be equally amazed at the way in which they come to life.

RIGHT *The fruit image is perfect for repoussé (see page 69) because it is simple but effective. It is also an ideal project for beginners because of its simplicity. The condiment and utensil holders were sealed with 6 coats of polyurethane hard varnish so that they will stand up to wear and tear.*

Serviettes

A whole new world was opened up to us when we stumbled across a range of new products which made decoupaging with serviettes so simple to do. The most exciting discovery for us is that it can be used on so many different surfaces.

Not only can you decorate wood, but also porcelain, glass, fabric, enamel and plastic. It is now possible to decorate a whole tea service for example, including cups, teapot, tablecloth and a tray, using the same range of serviettes.

Remember the days when you had sheets and sheets of gift wrap stuffed into drawers and cupboards and never had to go out and buy paper to wrap a present because you had a better collection than the shops? It's now time to make some more space because the same thing is going to happen – this time with serviettes.

It's advisable to use good-quality serviettes because the paper is stronger and the colours more intense so, even though it's more expensive than using gift wrap, a pack of serviettes goes a long way. We suggest you set up some sort of 'serviette club' and trade your left-overs with each other because unless you've got really carried away and decoupaged virtually everything in sight, you will have too many in the same range.

You could, of course, simply use them in the manner they were intended and always have a collection of interesting serviettes for entertaining! Some craft shops and hardware stores have cottoned-on to the increased interest in this form of decoupage and supply smaller packs of serviettes specifically for this purpose.

This is also one form of decoupage where wrinkles are not your enemy. In some instances, wrinkling actually enhances the finish, giving it a more textured and 'Eastern' look.

We have divided this section into various sub-sections because the techniques vary slightly depending on the surface on which you're working. Don't be afraid to experiment and break a few traditional decoupage rules.

LEFT *We could have sold this set ten times over! It is a good combination of almost all the serviette techniques discussed in this section. The vases were covered with an entire serviette glued directly onto the raw wood (only a base coat of Podge was applied). The insides of the vases were polished with shoe polish instead of being painted. Various sections of the serviette were then cut out to be applied to the porcelain and fabric. Ensure that any oriental writing is placed the right way round in case you have visitors from the Far East coming over for dinner!*

Cutting techniques

Opposite page We bought these beautiful serviettes on one of our business trips. We didn't have a specific project in mind but months later came across the wooden lamp base and immediately the elephant serviettes sprung to mind. Luckily they fitted perfectly around the base of the lamp. The lamp was painted with 4 coats of broken-white PVA followed by a simple wash of raw-sienna and raw-umber artist's acrylic.

Below We bought this inexpensive magazine stand and gave it an olive makeover. Unfortunately we forgot to wash it first and the images started lifting after about a month. This was easily rectified by applying another coat of serviette medium over the olives and re-ironing it. But this would not have been necessary had we washed the fabric beforehand.

The approach here is similar to cutting paper but the serviettes are so delicate that you need to work with a gentler hand. It may take some time to perfect, but it really isn't difficult. We have found that when you cut serviettes with a craft knife, the blades become blunt very quickly and, because it is imperative that you use a razor-sharp blade, you'll find that you'll go through blades a lot quicker than you normally would. We therefore suggest that you use a pair of manicure or small, comfortable embroidery scissors for as much of the cutting as possible.

Should you find it much easier to cut with a knife, simply ensure that you have spare blades on hand.

We prefer not to seal the serviette with Podge before cutting because it causes the serviette to wrinkle, making application more difficult.

1 Remove the back layer of the serviette. Most good-quality serviettes have three layers and it is only necessary to cut through two. If you attempt to cut through three it can become troublesome and, worse still, the blade on your craft knife will quickly become blunt.

2 Cut out the picture, remembering to cut away the inside bits first and then the outer edges last. If you are using a craft knife be careful not to drag the blade and tear the serviette. Press firmly into the serviette rather than pulling the blade along it.

3 Separate the last two layers as only the top layer is used. If you have difficulty separating the layers insert the blade of a craft knife between them. This will help you to find a loose edge.

Serviettes on fabric

We have found that pre-shrunk, bleached calico or seed cloth is the most practical fabric on which to decoupage with serviettes. It's inexpensive and works very well. It can be used for cushion covers, table cloths, bed linen, placemats and many other utility items. Other natural fabrics can be used but stay away from ones that have been pre-treated with a synthetic substance such as Teflon, for instance. As serviettes are very transparent, the colour of the fabric will show through the serviette, therefore light coloured fabrics give the best results. To change the background colour, the fabric can be painted with fabric paint and heat-sealed before decoupaging it.

LEFT *You are going to have to haul our your sewing machine or find a friend who sews once you start applying serviettes to fabric. Luckily, it's not difficult to sew a tablecloth (even Tracy could manage this one!) and the ivy finished it off perfectly. Remember to hem the cloth before applying the serviette.*

RIGHT *If you don't want to sew items yourself, there are plenty of plain fabric ones available (like this bag) which can be painted or left natural before being decorated.*

YOU WILL NEED

YOU WILL NEED

Plastic sheeting

Fabric

Serviette – cut and separated

Water-soluble fabric marker (blue or purple colour)

Fabric/textile medium

Flat soft synthetic brush

1 Put a plastic sheet underneath the fabric to protect the working surface and then decide where you're going to place the cut-out. Lay it down in position and, using a water-soluble fabric pen, make marks on the fabric around and slightly beyond the image.

2 Apply textile medium liberally to the fabric, covering the whole area up to the markings.

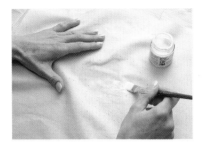

3 Start applying the serviette to the fabric by gently placing one edge of the picture onto the moistened area and begin brushing it down lightly using extra medium. Work towards the middle and then over to the opposite side, until the whole image is smoothed down. Ensure that the medium is extended slightly further than the picture to ensure that the edges don't lift. Leave to dry.

4 Brush on a second coat of textile medium. Don't worry about the appearance – you won't see the medium once it dries. Allow to dry for approximately four hours.

5 Heat-seal the picture onto the fabric by covering it with a cloth and ironing it (we recommend a cotton-temperature setting) for approximately three minutes. Be careful not to hold the iron in one position for too long otherwise you'll scorch the picture. Iron the fabric on the reverse side as well unless it's impossible (a plastic-backed lampshade cannot be ironed, try a hair-dryer). Once you have finished, you will notice that the serviette has 'melted' into the fabric.

'WRINKLE-FREE' METHOD

Those of you who really don't like the wrinkles that are almost impossible to avoid when applying a sizeable serviette cut-out, can use the following method to overcome this problem:

- Get hold of some non-woven, double-sided, iron-on interfacing which is available at most fabric shops. Iron the interfacing onto the back of the serviette before cutting.
- Cut out the image and peel off the backing paper.
- Iron the cut-out into position on your fabric in order to 'glue' it into place.

- Brush on one coat of serviette medium over the serviette (ensuring you don't miss any bits), taking the medium slightly beyond the cut out.
- When dry, place a piece of fabric over the image and iron once more to ensure that it is heat-sealed properly.

It is worth trying this method of applying serviettes in order to decide which 'look' you prefer. We've found that the end result is slightly more 'rubbery' when using interfacing but less medium is used and it is a perfect way to decorate children's T-shirts.

- Only use a synthetic brush as a natural-fibre brush will tear the serviette.
- Any raised 'dots' on the border of the serviette will flatten and disappear when ironed.

- A little bit of water will take away any remaining pen markings.
- The cloth is hand-washable in lukewarm water. Don't use strong washing powders or bleach and don't rub the fabric together otherwise a stone-washed effect will occur.
- Do not tumble dry or dry clean.
- If any edges have lifted, reapply the medium, wait for it to dry and heat-seal again.
- Lighter fabrics are more suitable

than darker ones as the image will simply disappear into darker colours.
- If you are placing a border onto your fabric, first hem the cloth.
- Serviettes stretch when being applied so make allowance for this when decorating a border.
- The fabric you are working with must be pre-shrunk.
- When ironing the fabric after use, always iron on the reverse side of the image, like you would a transfer.
- Don't use steam when ironing over the serviette the first time.

LEFT *For this border pattern we overlapped the serviettes slightly so that the joins would not be obvious. Every second serviette was turned over and applied in reverse in order to line up the joined sections.*

LEFT *The plain cotton rug was given a face-lift by decorating the edges with shells. The serviettes moulded well onto the textured surfaces of both the rug and the slippers. Fabric medium was used on the laundry bag and rug, while we used lacquer medium for the slippers.*

RIGHT *Inexpensive bleached calico was used to make these placemats. As the images are bright and bold they worked well on the calico. The breadbasket was colourwashed with white paint before being decorated with the same serviettes. A layer of polyurethane varnish was used over the entire basket to protect the paint finish and the images.*

Serviettes on porcelain, glass and enamel

BELOW *The canisters' lids had to be redone as the bubbles went darker on them than on the bases when baked. This happened because the lids got hotter a lot quicker than the bases owing to their size. It was easy to rectify and the lids were then baked for half as long as the bases.*

Finding a medium which enables you to decoupage onto these surfaces and then actually being able to use the finished item rather than having something purely decorative felt, to us, like the invention of washing-machines must have felt to our grandmothers (or mothers – depending on your age!). As the serviette is so thin, it is also a lot easier to mould onto a curved surface than paper. The same theory applies as to fabric – a lighter background is preferable to a darker one otherwise the image will get 'lost'. You will be amazed at how quickly a tea service can be decorated as there is no painting involved!

1 Clean the item with methylated spirits and leave to dry. Place the cut-out in the position that you want it and hold it there with one hand. Begin applying the porcelain medium by brushing it onto the serviette from one side to the other, ensuring that your brush is always fairly wet. A light brush stroke is needed to avoid tearing the serviette. Extend the medium slightly beyond the image.

2 Wipe away any excess medium from around the edges of the cut-out with a cloth dampened with methylated spirits, taking care not to disturb the serviette in the process. Leave to dry for about four hours.

BELOW *The colour of the serviettes darkened slightly after being baked in the oven to heat seal.*

YOU WILL NEED
Porcelain, glass or enamel item
Methylated spirits
Serviette – cut and separated
Porcelain medium
Flat soft synthetic brush
Soft cloth

3 Preheat the oven to a temperature of 170 °C. Once the oven has reached its temperature, bake the porcelain for 30 minutes (reduce this to 15–20 minutes for enamel because metal heats up quicker than porcelain). Take it out and leave it to cool down. The baking almost 'melts' the serviette image onto the item you have decorated.

- These items can be washed in lukewarm water, but they are not dishwasher safe.
- Item must be baked in a conventional oven and not in a microwave oven.
- Be careful not to touch the serviette whilst it is still wet otherwise it will lift and tear.
- Any dry excess medium that you have missed when cleaning around the serviettes can be scratched away carefully prior to baking, using a blade.
- If any sides of the cut-out lift because you have not applied the medium correctly, simply re-apply medium and re-bake.
- Decorate plates on the outer rim only – not on the cutting area, as the serviette will eventually become damaged.
- If you are decorating a salt and pepper set don't put them in the oven without first removing the little plastic stoppers underneath.
- The colours on the serviette darken after being baked. This is not really noticeable with dark colours but whites end up looking as if they have been tea-stained. The longer you leave the item in the oven, the darker the colours become. It is for this precise reason that we have cut down on 'baking time' after having experimented.
- If at any time after you have baked the item, you wish to get rid of the decorations, simply soak it for about 40 minutes in hot water and then scrape away the cut-outs with a blade. Hold the blade as flat as you can against the porcelain or enamel to avoid scratching the surface. If the images are still difficult to remove, brush either thinners or methylated spirits over them before continuing with the blade. Rub the whole item down with methylated spirits or thinners once images are removed. (Please remember that thinners is extremely powerful and can eat into varnish and painted surfaces, so take care when using it. It is also not a good idea to sniff or drink the stuff!)

RIGHT *An entire serviette was used to cover the sides of these glass containers. The serviette had a white background which became transparent once the serviette medium was applied to it. This gives the impression that the intricate images were cut out. The wooden lids were painted dark green to match the serviette.*

SERVIETTES ON WOOD

The beauty of using serviettes on painted wood is that they are thin and are very similar to working with transfers. You don't need many layers of varnish to bury the picture. Bear in mind that the background colour will show through the serviette as with a transfer so, unless you want a really muted effect, choose a light background colour. By using the entire serviette and covering the object completely, a textured effect can be achieved which is just as well as it is virtually impossible to apply a whole serviette without wrinkles.

BELOW *These images were taken from a Christmas theme serviette, though you would never know it because anything relating to Christmas was cut away. So don't ignore 'theme' serviettes, they can be adapted.*

YOU WILL NEED
Raw-wood item
Broken-white PVA base coat
Woodfiller
400-grit sandpaper
Acrylic or PVA paint in colour of
    your choice
Modge Podge
Serviette – cut and separated
Water-based polyurethane
    hard varnish/lacquer medium
Flat soft synthetic brush

1 Apply a base coat of broken-white PVA to the object and leave to dry. Fill any holes or blemishes with wood filler and sand with 400-grit sandpaper when dry. Paint the item with desired colour (at least four coats). Apply one coat of Modge Podge and leave to dry.

2 Arrange cut-outs onto the wood in order to get a good idea of how the finished item will look. Once you are happy with the arrangement begin gluing the cut-out into position by brushing the medium onto the serviette, working from one side to the other. Extend the medium slightly beyond the cut-out to ensure adhesion. Allow to dry for 20 to 40 minutes.

3 Apply four to six coats of medium or varnish to the whole item to finish it off, allowing each coat to dry before applying the next one.

RIGHT *The serviette used on the clock was given to us by a student who got it from a restaurant in America. We had to make sure that we didn't make any mistakes because we had only one serviette! Once the background was painted and the serviette glued down, the entire clock was crackled. The cracks were filled with burnt umber oil-paint and when dry, the clock was sealed with 3 coats of oil-based varnish.*

HANDY HINTS

- When covering an item completely with a serviette, after you have applied the medium dab the serviette down with a damp cloth in order to remove any air bubbles.
- Serviettes can be moulded over and around any routed edges.
- Resin may also be used as a final finish as long as you've sealed the item with about five coats of medium before pouring the resin.
- It's also possible to use Modge Podge instead of the abovementioned mediums as a final finish, but only if you have applied the serviette with it.
- A slightly distressed, worn effect can be achieved by sanding lightly over the serviette once it has been stuck down (and is dry!). Use 400 grit sandpaper.
- Images can be reversed by actually reversing the cut-out – you use the serviette the wrong way around. Once the medium has been applied, you'll see that the colour comes right through the reverse side.

ABOVE *When looking for a serviette to decorate this tea box our first thoughts were of tea cups until we found these paisley serviettes. For some reason the design reminded us of the East (although paisley originated in Scotland!). We covered the box completely with serviettes and cut out one of the images to be placed on the porcelain tea set. The serviette was moulded over the lid of the box and applied to the individual dividers inside the box for a truly professional finish.*

THREE-DIMENSIONAL DECOUPAGE USING SERVIETTES

We decided to include this chapter because serviettes are becoming increasingly popular as source materials. The two most requested techniques these days are three-dimensional and serviette decoupage and so it obviously makes sense to try to combine the two in some way. There are two methods we use to create height with serviettes that involve similar techniques to the ones described in the chapters on three-dimensional decoupage (see pages 59-71). For paper tole, the same method is used (see page 65) except that the serviette is prepared as explained in the box below.

However, when using clay to create height, the technique varies quite considerably from repoussé so for this reason we have chosen to explain this method in detail.

It is a lot quicker (and easier!) to do than repoussé and the completed, raised image can either be left flat so that it looks like it has been cut out of wood, or moulded slightly, which gives the impression of pottery.

Once again, we have experimented with various ways of executing this technique and have described to you what we consider to be the easiest and most effective.

LEFT It was wonderful to be able to combine three-dimensional and serviette decoupage in one project. Once completed the images on this CD box looked like simple carved wooden ones. We didn't mould them at all because we wanted a flat look but it would look equally effective to add the odd indentation here and there.

SERVIETTES FOR PAPER TOLE

The use of serviettes for paper tole is almost identical to using prints or giftwrap (see page 65), the only difference being that the serviettes need to be glued (using a water-based polyurethane varnish or lacquer medium) onto stiffer paper before you can begin your project.

The best way of doing this is to place the serviette onto plain white paper and then apply a layer of varnish over it. The varnish is absorbed through the serviette onto the paper thereby gluing it into place. Leave it to dry completely before beginning to cut and remember that at least five copies of the same image are needed.

YOU WILL NEED

Raw-wood item

Broken-white PVA coat

Woodfiller

400-grit sandpaper

Acrylic or PVA paint colour of your
choice

Modge Podge

White air-hardening modeling clay

Plastic cling wrap

Rolling pin

Serviette – cut and separated

Flat soft synthetic brush/foam
applicator

Water-based polyurethane hard
varnish/lacquer medium

Craft knife

Cutting mat

Paper moulding tool or nail
cuticle set

White wood-glue

1 Apply a base coat of broken-white PVA to the object and leave to dry. Fill any holes or blemishes with wood filler and sand with 400-grit sandpaper when dry. Paint the item with desired colour. Apply one coat of Modge Podge and leave to dry.

2 Place a piece of clay between two pieces of cling wrap and roll it out flat as you would pastry. It can be as thick or as thin as you want

it, although we don't recommend making it less than 3 mm because the finished look is not very effective.

3 Remove the cling wrap and place the serviette cut-out onto the clay. Once it is in position, begin gluing it down by brushing medium or varnish over the serviette, working from one side to the other. Extend the medium slightly beyond the cut-out to ensure good adherence. Allow the varnish to dry, but not the clay. We recommend leaving it for about an hour.

4 Carefully cut away the excess clay from around the image using a craft knife. Cut down firmly and try not to drag the knife. If the clay feels a little too 'mushy', leave it for half and hour and come back to it.

5 Use the moulding tool or manicure set to neaten the clay edges. This is made easier by dipping the tool into water every now and again as you move around the edges because the water helps to smooth the clay.

6 Apply white wood-glue to the underside of the finished clay cut-out and press it gently into position on the prepared item, squeezing out the excess glue from underneath as you do so. Be careful not to dent the clay cut-out with fingers. Clean away the glue from the sides and use the moulding tool to fix any edges that may have been damaged in the gluing process. Place the item on a flat surface with the image face upwards and leave to dry.

7 Once both the glue and the clay are dry, paint the edges of the image with either the same colour PVA as the box or mix a colour to match the serviette. When dry, apply four to six coats of medium or varnish to the whole item to finish it off, allowing each coat to dry before applying the next one.

HANDY HINTS

- If you discover that you've placed the image in the wrong position after gluing, remove it before the glue dries by carefully sliding a blunt-edged knife underneath it to lift it up. There should be enough glue underneath for you to reposition it without having to add more.
- Once the glue has dried you can use the moulding tool or manicure set to press in any details, like petals or drapes in clothing. Make sure that the tool that you are using is blunt, otherwise you will tear the serviette. Don't use anything with a point and don't press too hard.
- The cut-out can also be glued onto a curved surface because

the clay is still wet, therefore it is flexible (that's why we don't leave it to dry before gluing).
- If you have glued onto a curved surface, it is still important to have the image facing upwards until it is dry, otherwise the weight of it will cause it to slide downwards. A good way to get around the problem of trying to balance a bowl or jar in an unnatural position is to use towels under and around it.
- This technique can be used to make fridge magnets as well. Instead of gluing the clay down onto a surface, simply leave it to dry, paint and varnish edges and underside and glue a magnet underneath.

ABOVE *The grey paint used on this box was left over after painting a lounge. It's a good way of using up left-over paint and at the same time, complimenting your décor. A dark blue paint was used on the edges to add interest to the box.*

Three-dimensional decoupage

Our first encounter with three-dimensional decoupage was during a course on repoussé with June Bisschop in 1997. A few years later we decided to attempt another form of three-dimensional work called 'paper tole'. We had one half-hour lesson on this and the rest was up to us. In our subsequent research, none of the literature that we came across went into any detail or was any help whatsoever regarding the cutting, which is a vital part of three-dimensional decoupage. Having spent a full week just on this particular section, we now know why – it really is incredibly hard to explain but not difficult to do! Read the instructions carefully and if you are still a little unsure, buy one of the pre-packed kits (available from craft shops and hardware stores) which mark out the cutting lines for you. Once you have completed one of them, everything we have explained will, hopefully, suddenly make perfect sense!

Unlike traditional decoupage which is flat, three-dimensional decoupage uses different mediums to raise the picture up from the surface (the third dimension is depth) to give a more vivid realism. This effect can be achieved by using either single or multiple prints. The two methods we will be concentrating on in this section are a form of paper tole and repoussé.

PREVIOUS PAGE *These boxes are ideal for storing silk scarves or special undergarments which have a habit of getting lost in clothes cupboards or sock drawers. The old-fashioned image gives it a romantic 1920s type feel. When building up the skirt of the 'Fallen Lady' we realized that we would have to cut it into sections first because the area was too large to work effectively in one piece. We therefore cut our own natural folds in the skirt, which also prevented it from looking too flat and boring.*

PAPER TOLE uses silicon adhesive to build up a picture by repeating and overlapping sections of the same image a number of times to create multiple levels. A more advanced technique is known as ELEVATION where, essentially, the picture is taken apart completely and then re-created. The images are only cut once and no double imagery is seen. For all intents and purposes elevation is a Guild standard of decoupage for master craftsmen and is not normally tackled by ordinary crafters, although once you have mastered

the art of paper tole and find that you enjoy it and want to go further, elevation is the next logical step.

REPOUSSÉ relies on the use of modelling clay to raise either a single or multiple images from the surface.

PAPERS & PRINTS

Any print or good quality gift-wrap is suitable for these techniques. As mentioned, pre-packed 3D kits are widely available and come with cutting guides and instructions. This is a good introduction to the technique and we suggest that you tackle one of these before breaking out on your own. If you'd rather use your own print or gift wrap though, please bear in mind that you'll need at least five copies of the same image (and this is where a colour photocopier comes in handy).

ABOVE *The chickens were cut from gift wrap and were a very cost effective way of producing paper-tole pictures, as only one sheet was needed. Once you have practised with a pack, it will be easy to do something like this on your own.*

Planning the design

This is one of the most important aspects of three-dimensional decoupage because it's where you decide which parts of the image will be in the foreground and which will remain in the background. Remember that you want to create a lifelike image so take into account which sections of the picture will be the farthest away and which will be nearer before beginning to cut. Now is also the time to decide whether to keep one print intact as a background to work from or whether to cut it away and work on a single image. An important thing to remember about planning the picture is that there is no right or wrong way to do it – it is all about how you perceive the picture. A couple of times we have built up the same image in two different ways – changing the order in which the pieces are laid – and both looked correct.

BELOW The box was first covered with torn pieces of brown paper which formed an interestingly textured background. The method used to repoussé these images was the quick-and-easy one, using only one print. The use of various coloured papers as a background, instead of painting, adds interest to your work.

CUTTING FOR PAPER TOLE & REPOUSSÉ

BELOW This was an extremely challenging yet satisfying picture to do. If you are a beginner we don't suggest that you attempt something like this as your first project. A lot of intricate cutting and bridging (see Handy Hints on page 35) was involved and cellophane was used in the shop windows to give it a more realistic look.

The secret to successful three-dimensional decoupage is to 'over-cut' the sections that you are going to use. In other words, cut slightly beyond the natural cutting line so that, when you lay on the next piece, no cutting edges are visible underneath – this just looks messy. The only time that you would cut exactly on the 'natural cutting line' is when it is not going to be overlapped by another part of the picture. Remember that neither the final piece (or pieces) nor the very first one (which is your base piece) will be over-cut. Before beginning to cut, refer to step one of the instructions on either repoussé or paper tole, depending on which technique you are following.

1 Cut out the image that is going to be used as the base print, in other words it will appear at the very back of your finished work. Label this piece number 1.

2 Using another print, decide what section should be built up next. Before you cut that section, work out what will be placed over or around it next. Once you are clear on this, 'over-cut' these areas. For example, we have cut the outer part of the bear's arm exactly on the cutting line because nothing will overlap it but have extended our cutting on the inside bits over his shirt, pants and foot. Remember it is not necessary to over-cut by too much otherwise you will find that you need more than the recommended 5 prints. Label this piece number 2 and lay it down, right side up, on top of the first cut-out in its correct place. This is a bit like preparing pieces for a puzzle!

3 Continuing with the bear, the next section to be cut is the bear's shirtsleeve. Use a new print for this – you cannot cut his sleeve from the print you have just been working on because of over-cutting. Don't throw away the previous print as you will need it again. Cut exactly on the outside cutting line and bottom edge of the bear's shirtsleeve, over-cutting into his epaulette and slightly into the main body of his shirt. Both the epaulette and shirt front will come on afterwards. Label this piece number 3 and add it to your puzzle, once again in the correct position.

4 Carry on in this fashion, using all four prints in order to cut the sections needed. You will find that you may, for example, have pieces number 2, 17, 14, 20, 10 and 16 cut out of one sheet and various other unconnected numbers cut out of another. This enables you to use the least number of prints possible. The final piece (or pieces) needed will not have to be over-cut because nothing is going to overlap them. It is imperative that you label each piece as you cut it, otherwise you will end up with a pile of cut outs and not know where to start! It is also a good idea to lay the pieces in their correct positions as you go along so that you can get a good idea in your mind of what the finished picture is going to look like. You can then decide whether or not you'll need to cut extras.

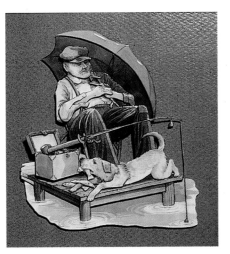

LEFT *When doing this project we made slits in the water section (at the bottom of the table legs) so that the legs could be tucked into the water rather than having them standing on top of it, adding to the three-dimensional look. Varnish was applied to the picture to give it a 'porcelain' finish.*

PAPER TOLE

While we were researching three-dimensional decoupage, it became apparent to us that what we all refer to as 3D is actually paper tole. We were still going to go ahead and call this section 3D to avoid confusion but Christopher (remember him – the nit-picking husband from the last book?) pointed out that all images that are raised up from the surface are three-dimensional anyway, and that we needed to be more specific. We eventually couldn't stand his interference anymore (and we do need him for the odd grammar correction) so we gave

in just to keep the peace. We have to admit that he is right though. So, welcome to paper tole (or 3D)!

PAPER TOLE is the art of cutting, moulding and gluing multiple cut-outs onto a background. We use clear silicon to glue the pieces into place. This enables you to control the height of various pieces by using more or less silicon. A number of people use double-sided sticky tape instead of silicon – particularly on greeting cards – but we prefer not to because it is not as easy to control the height and the tape is often more visible.

OPPOSITE PAGE Children love clowns and they are really fun to work on. Once this one was completed we snipped away some of the excess 'double imagery' behind the umbrella handle and ring. Be sure to ask whoever frames your pictures to make the frame deep enough to ensure the picture doesn't press up against the glass. This can easily happen and will ruin your finished work.

BELOW These fun cards are a brilliant way of saving money on greeting cards. The images were cut out from inexpensive gift wrap and then built up. Teach your children how to make their own paper tole greeting cards – they will love it!

YOU WILL NEED

5 or more copies of your picture
    of choice
Foam applicator
Modge Podge
Mounting board – approximately
    10 cm wider and longer than
    the print
Paper or wood glue
Cutting mat
Craft knife or emboidery scissors
Pencil
Watercolour paints
Small paint brush
Moulding tool or manicure set
Tube of clear silicon
Toothpicks
Paper glue or white wood-glue
Daler-Rowney's Poster and Water-
    colour Varnish (optional)

1 Using a foam applicator, apply a thin coat of Modge Podge to all the prints you wish to use. If you are using gift wrap or any other thinner paper, apply a coat to the back as well for added protection. It's also a good idea to seal the mounting board in the same manner to protect it from finger marks and silicon blunders. Bear in mind though that it will darken slightly when sealed. Leave to dry.

2 If there is a flat background to your picture, this needs to be trimmed (if necessary) and glued down onto the mounting board using paper glue or watered-down wood glue – about 2 parts glue to 1 part water. (If there is no background to the picture, no gluing is necessary yet). Allow to dry.

3 Re-read the sections on planning the design and cutting techniques for three-dimensional decoupage before starting to cut. Decide which piece needs to be placed first, cut it out with a craft knife or manicure scissors and number it on the reverse side. At this point you can continue cutting all the pieces you will need to complete your picture or you can cut as you go along. Remember to number the pieces.

4 Carefully paint all white edges of the cut-outs with thin water-colour paints. This gives the finished work a professional, more realistic look. Leave to dry.

5 Shape each piece before mounting it to create a more realistic effect. Place the cut-out on a soft cloth and, using a moulding tool (or part of your manicure set), rub in

small circular movements around the edges of the cut-out. Study the individual pieces that you are working with – some may need folding or creasing before mounting for a realistic three-dimensional look.

6 Take the first cut-out to be mounted (remember you're working from background to foreground) and turn it over. Squeeze out a small blob of silicon and scrape it off the top of the tube with a toothpick. Place both the toothpick and silicon down onto the back of the cut-out (about 3 mm from the edge) and gently roll the toothpick in your fingers. The silicon should remain in a round blob on the cut-out and you will be able to pull the toothpick free. Continue applying blobs of silicon all the way around the cut-out with a spacing of about 1 cm between them. A larger cut-out will need blobs placed in the middle as well, for extra support.

7 Carefully pick up the cut-out (use a pair of tweezers for this, especially the small, fiddly bits), avoiding touching the silicon in the process, and place it into position on the mounting board. Lay it down gently and press ever so slightly on it to affix it.

8 Prepare and mount the next piece in the same manner, making sure that it's lined up correctly. We prefer to continue working on the whole design in one sitting (provided it isn't one of the more complicated ones) because the silicon takes a while to dry and pieces can be moved slightly if necessary while the silicon is still wet. The drawback of doing it this way is that you have to work very carefully to avoid shifting pieces, although it's not as difficult as it sounds.

9 Once the picture is complete, leave it to dry overnight. You can then leave it as is or varnish it to give it a porcelain-like appearance. Use only the recommended Poster and Water-colour varnish as it doesn't run if applied properly. Apply it from a fabric painting bottle that has a nozzle. The best way to do it is to make little dots of varnish all over the picture, working on one section at a time. The dots need to be pretty close to each other so that they can join together to give even coverage. Hold the work up to the light and check for any unvarnished bits and bubbles. Bubbles can be removed with a toothpick while gaps can be fixed with an extra dot of varnish. Leave the varnished picture on a flat surface in a dust-free environment to dry. You can cover it if you like but don't put it in a plastic bag (it may stick to the varnish). Apply another coat of varnish for a really professional finish. We prefer to wait four days before doing this because sometimes the first coat is not completely dry and by putting on another coat too soon, you run the risk of having a permanently-tacky piece of work.

HANDY HINTS

- If you come across images that you wish to use that are too thin (such as serviettes) glue them onto firmer paper before mounting using serviette medium.
- Once the work is complete, you may decide that some of the thinner sections have too much 'double imagery' – the extra sections underneath can be snipped away carefully with a pair of manicure scissors.
- Any silicon messes should be cleaned up as you go along. If they have dried simply scrape them away very carefully with a blunt-edged knife (provided you have sealed the mounting board beforehand).
- Be careful when applying new sections, not to lean on the ones just done – you will flatten them and spoil the effect.
- Should you find that a piece has been positioned incorrectly (and has already dried), you can simply slice through the silicon with a craft knife and re-glue it.

REPOUSSÉ

This is a French word which, roughly translated into English, means 'to raise or push up'. We've also seen it referred to as 'moulage' (another French word meaning 'casting' or 'plaster cast'). Whichever term you want to use, though, it looks like we can blame the French if your project doesn't work!

Repoussé is a form of three-dimensional decoupage which builds up the picture from the surface by using a solid filling. Various 'building' materials can be used: papier-mâché or salt dough, for instance, but they're messy and difficult to work with. We recommend building the picture up with air-hardening modelling clay instead, which is placed underneath the cut-outs before they're glued down in place. The image can then be moulded because of the clay. The effect is a little more subtle than paper tole and the technique more versatile. It can be done on virtually any flat or curved surface. But don't try it on a tray as the cups tend to fall over!

Repoussé can be as involved or simple as you want to make it. You can approach it in the same way that you would paper tole, by building up various sections at a time, or you can take the simple, quick-and-easy approach and build up a single cut-out. The single cut-out is only really suitable for smaller images because the larger the cut-out, the more chance you have of trapping air under it, which leads to difficulty in moulding. That is why, if you want to repoussé a larger image, it's better to work in sections, even creating your own sections where there aren't obvious ones already, as we did on the hat boxes (see page 58).

LEFT This plate was our first attempt at repoussé and we thought it was awfully clever! The figures were built up individually and there were plenty of drapes to practise our moulding skills on.

BELOW Images depicting any type of 'draping' are perfect for repoussé because it is easy to mould the garments and they look particularly effective when done.

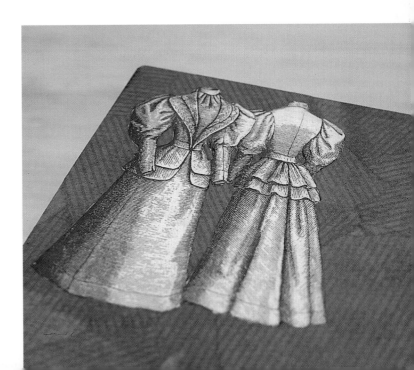

REPOUSSÉ USING MULTIPLE LAYERS

YOU WILL NEED

5 or more copies of the picture you
  wish to repoussé

Modge Podge

Foam applicator

Box

Broken-white PVA paint

Wood filler

400-grit sandpaper

Acrylic craft paint

Cutting mat

Craft knife or manicure scissors

Pencil

White wood-glue

White air-hardening modelling clay

Kitchen wipes

Paper-moulding tool
  or manicure set

Toothpicks

White vinegar

Watercolour paints

Thin paintbrush

Varnish

1 Using a foam applicator, apply six coats of Modge Podge onto all copies of the picture you wish to use, allowing drying time in between coats. When dry, apply another six coats onto the back of the images as well, to waterproof the paper and prevent it from tearing when you work with it. Allow to dry.

2 Apply a base coat of broken-white PVA to your box and leave to dry. Fill any holes or blemishes with filler and sand with 400-grit sandpaper when dry. Paint it with the desired colour (at least four coats). Apply one coat of Modge Podge and leave to dry.

3 Re-read the section on planning the design and cutting techniques (see pages 61–63). Carefully study the image, decide what needs to be placed down first and cut it out with a craft knife (or scissors). We cut all the necessary pieces before sticking them down; you can cut as you go along if you find it easier. Remember to number the pieces.

4 Glue the first image which will be your base into place, using slightly watered-down wood glue – about 2 parts glue to 1 part water. Make sure that there are no air bubbles and leave to dry.

5 Take the next piece to be used working from background to foreground and place it face down on a damp kitchen wipe. Apply undiluted wood glue to the entire back of the picture – enough to cover it, not drown it. Make tiny 'sausages' of clay and place them at regular intervals over the glue. A little goes a long way, so don't overdo it.

6 Press down on the clay sausages with the back of the moulding tool. The clay needs to be spread evenly over the entire cut-out. Once you have got it as smooth as possible, apply another layer of wood glue over the clay, once again not too much! Leave for about five minutes to become slightly tacky (otherwise it won't stick). A good rule to remember is 'glue-clay-glue'.

7 Lift up the cut-out with the clay on it, turn it over and place it into position on the base print. Using the moulding tool, begin pressing down firmly on the edges in order to secure them. Some of the clay will

now squeeze out of the edges. As you work, remove any clay and glue that may have oozed out (a toothpick is a useful tool here). If you have a section that was 'over-cut' remove all the clay from underneath this portion by pressing it out because this particular section will be built up later.

Continue in this way until all pieces have been placed. (You will not be able to work over pieces that are still wet, therefore allow drying time before continuing).

8 Each piece needs about one hour of drying time before it can be moulded effectively. Using the moulding tool, make definite lines in the picture to make it lifelike. For instance you can accentuate the creased lines on the shirt of the bear, the pin on the tie, the mouth and paws. Be careful not to get too carried away and mould too much. A subtle effect is better than some wrinkled image! Clean the entire (dry) surface with a little vinegar water to remove any leftover glue or finger marks.

9 Using a thin paintbrush and watercolour paints, paint the edges in order to cover up any white bits that may be showing. Allow to dry and then seal with four to six coats of varnish of your choice, allowing it to dry completely between coats.

HANDY HINTS

- Don't stack your pictures one on top of the other once you've podged both sides – they'll stick together.
- Images filled with clay shrink slightly, so it's advisable to cut the base picture slightly smaller where you will be overlapping to avoid double imagery.
- It's essential to clean away any excess glue and clay as you work – the clay dries hard and is almost impossible to remove once dry.
- Take care when applying new sections not to lean on those just done – you'll flatten them.
- Combining flat and repousséd images in your work gives an interesting effect.

- A thin stem can be virtually impossible to glue down with clay underneath; leave it flat or build it up by sticking another identical stem over it to give it height.
- Little pieces, such as buttons, can be added in the final stages. Simply glue them on. No clay is necessary and you will still get the impression of depth.
- In order to prolong the 'life' of your unused clay, don't expose it to air too much. While working with it, remember to seal it if you go away and do something else. We keep ours sealed in a plastic bag once it's been opened. It's also a good idea to keep this bag in the fridge when you're not using the clay.

REPOUSSÉ USING A SINGLE LAYER

The technique used for applying a single layer is much the same as for multiple layers except that you use only one image and omit the base print. Clay and glue are applied to the single cut-out and this is stuck down directly onto the surface you are decoupaging. Clean up and mould the image in exactly the same way as you would for multiple-layering.

Luminaire

RIGHT *The hurricane lamp looks completely different once decorated and displayed with a lit candle inside. The advantage of using serviettes instead of normal paper cut-outs for luminaire is that the lamp or glass item can be viewed from any angle and there is no wrong side to the image.*

BELOW *We wanted the hurricane lamps to compliment each other but didn't have the correct colour mulberry paper to achieve this effect, so out come the tea and coffee, which was used to stain the white paper before we applied it. The use of a similar coloured serviette pine cone on the white lamp brought the whole set together.*

Luminaires are an attractive way of lighting a room by using inexpensive glassware and a decoupage-on-glass technique. Handmade mulberry paper is used to achieve a soft romantic look which is further enhanced by a lit candle placed inside the glass item. As this technique is quick and easy, you can transform a rather ordinary dinner table into something special in a hurry. It is a great way of creating a theme for a special occasion, such as a dinner party or an anniversary celebration.

You can extend this technique to any glass item such as a vase or decorative plate. The vase can be used to hold fresh flowers in water as only the outside of the vase will be decorated. The glass item can be decorated further by placing cut-out images onto the mulberry paper. We recommend using either serviettes or transfers for this purpose, otherwise a solid white image will be seen from the inside of the glass. Serviettes and transfers are delicate enough to allow light to shine through and the image is visible from inside and out. As the mulberry paper is already textured don't over-decorate!

Mulberry paper is obtainable from many stationery and craft shops but you'll find that it comes in different weights: make sure that you ask for the very thin paper (almost like tissue paper) as it's the only type suitable for this technique.

Mulberry paper is sometimes referred to as rice paper but it depends on the country that you are in at the time and the manufacturer's idea of what to call it.

YOU WILL NEED

Glass object

Handmade mulberry paper

Water-based, heat-resistant
  varnish

Foam applicator

Soft cloth

Transfer, or cut-outs from a
  serviette

Kitchen wipe

Craft knife

Glitter glue (optional)

Small floating candle

1 Wash and dry glass well. Tear mulberry paper into small pieces (about 3 cm by 3 cm) but don't try to tear perfect squares: it is not necessary and it looks better if they aren't identical. Do not cut, as straight edges do not blend well. Straight edges are only used on the rim of the glass to avoid excess trimming.

2 Apply a fair amount of varnish over a section of the glass with an applicator. Place one piece of mulberry paper onto the varnished area and work in more varnish over the paper by dabbing at it with the applicator until it's completely wet.

3 Continue working in this fashion, overlapping pieces slightly as you go along. Remember to apply varnish to each section of glass before laying down and working the paper. Don't worry about the odd crease – just dab it down with your applicator. Carry on in this way until the whole area that you wish to cover is done.

4 Dab firmly with a damp cloth to remove any excess varnish and bubbles. Check from the inside of the glass (they're easier to spot this way) for any missed places and patch if necessary. Allow to dry. Don't forget to turn over the glass and apply mulberry paper to the underside as well. There's no need to worry about excess paper extending over the edges as this will be trimmed later. Leave to dry.

5 Using a craft knife, trim away any excess paper from around the rim and base of the glass. You might need to neaten the area around the stem. If so, this can also be done with a craft

knife. Rub glitter glue around the rim and on the base of the glass if you want a slightly more ornate look or are working with a Christmas theme.

6 Place cut out pictures into position on the glass over the mulberry paper using the varnish as an adhesive. If you are applying a serviette cut-out, gently brush varnish over the top of the dry serviette to glue it into position (working from one side to the other). If you are using a transfer, place it on a kitchen wipe and apply varnish to the reverse side before gluing it into place.

7 Allow to dry and apply an even coat of varnish to the entire area that you've covered and decorated. Apply a further three coats allowing drying time between each one. To use, fill the glass a quarter full with water and float a small, round-based candle.

RIGHT *Wine-glass luminaires make attractive centre pieces for a table setting. We felt that the blue was a beautiful vibrant colour and needed no further decorating other than a little silver glitter on the rims of the glasses. The white luminaire was decorated with cut-out images from a serviette. Half-fill the glasses with water in order to float a candle inside of them.*

- Ensure that the wine glass you use has a wide top, otherwise the heat from the candle could crack it (no champagne flutes).
- If you want an even more muted light, use a single, plain serviette layer over the mulberry paper and image. This can be applied in torn strips down the length of the glass (using the same method as you've used for the mulberry paper).
- We've noticed that delicate images go much better with this soft look than bulky ones.
- Clean the decorated glass with a damp cloth. Never immerse it in water.
- On the other hand, if you become tired of your decorated glass or wish to change the theme, don't throw it away. Simply soak it in very hot, soapy water for an hour or two and you will be able to peel off the paper. Now simply wipe it clean, and redecorate.
- When you are decorating a number of wine glasses for a table setting, leave some without images to prevent the setting from looking over-done.
- If you want to put pictures or glitter on the base of the glass, do this before applying the mulberry paper so that it will be visible through the base.

BREA

Using fabric

Your cupboards are now overflowing with gift wrap and ser-viettes and your spouse is probably thinking, "Surely it has to stop now?". Not a hope! It's now time to find even more space for fabric off-cuts.

Fabric decoupage can be done on galvanized steel, papier-mâché, cardboard and even ostrich eggs (although we don't know why you would want to do this!). Basically, anything that can be decoupaged with paper can be de-coupaged with fabric as well.

By using this simple technique you can now make a bread bin to match your kitchen curtains, a wastepaper bin to match a bedspread, or a CD box to match the duvet-cover in your daughter's bedroom. The images on the fabric can either be cut out or an uncut piece can be used to cover an item completely.

In this chapter we decided to stick with 'fun' fabrics but classic designs also work well. What we've found from ex-perience is that cotton or cotton-mix fabrics are the easiest to work with. Many people are concerned that the fabric is going to fray. Don't worry: as long as the fabric has been sealed properly this won't happen.

LEFT *The bright, bold images of this fabric worked very well on the bread bin. The wording on the bread bin was dabbed on over a stencil (which was made out of and old X-ray). This is a good way of matching the decor in your kitchen.*

YOU WILL NEED

Wooden blank
Broken-white PVA base coat
Wood filler
400-grit sandpaper
Acrylic or PVA paint in colour of
  your choice
Sponge applicator
Modge Podge
Fabric
Craft knife or scissors
Cutting mat
Prestik (blue tac)
White wood-glue or fabric glue
Rubber roller
Varnish of your choice
Soft cloth

1 Apply a base coat of broken-white PVA to the item and leave to dry. Fill any holes with wood filler and sand with 400-grit sandpaper when dry. Paint your item with your choice of colour (at least four coats). Allow to dry and apply one coat of Modge Podge. Leave to dry.

2 Using a sponge applicator, seal the fabric on both sides with a generous amount of Modge Podge, allowing the first side to dry before doing the other. Extend the Modge Podge slightly beyond the image.

3 Cut out the images using a craft knife or a pair of scissors. The fabric is really easy to cut once it has been sealed.

4 Arrange cut-outs on the wood in order to get an idea of what the finished item will look like. A little Prestik can be used to hold them in place. Once you're happy with the arrangement you can begin to glue using white wood-glue or fabric glue. Apply glue to the back of the cut-outs (one piece at a time) and roll into place with a rubber roller, making sure that all wrinkles and air bubbles are smoothed out.

5 Clean away any excess glue with a damp cloth and ensure that all edges are firmly glued down. Leave to dry.

6 Apply at least six coats of water-based varnish to the entire item, allowing sufficient drying time between coats.

LEFT We stumbled across this hot-air balloon in a fabric sample book. The shape of the balloon fitted perfectly on the umbrella stand. We recreated the background colour of the fabric onto the wood because it worked well with the balloon. The background was painted crème caramel and then dabbed with a slightly darker shade of the same colour. Metallic gold paint was used to finish off the edges (to Geoff's delight) and 6 coats of oil-based varnish completed the project.

- When cutting out an image from a piece of fabric, cut slightly inside of the natural cutting line to avoid any background showing on the cut-out.
- When covering an item completely – apply the glue directly onto the surface that you are decorating rather than to the fabric. Trim away any excess fabric from the sides when dry.
- Ensure that you do not use 'quickset wood-glue', especially if gluing larger pieces of fabric.
- Should you wish to finish off with resin, apply at least eight coats of Modge Podge before pouring the resin, otherwise it will seep into the fabric and ruin the images.
- A good idea is to cover a box completely with fabric (like a stripe or a check) and then glue a fabric cut-out over that.

BELOW *The pine frame of this set was painted with diluted white paint. The table top and chair bases were painted with two shades of blue which were blended together while the paint was still wet. The lettering on the chairs was cut from the fabric using a craft knife and each letter was glued down individually. You could personalise the chairs by stencilling children's names on them. The items were all finished off with 6 coats of polyurethane varnish to make them more hard-wearing.*

Candles

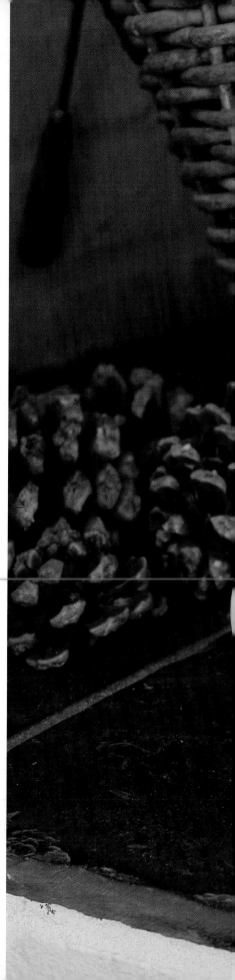

Gone are the days when the only candles in the house were those ones shoved in the back of a drawer and only hauled out when the electricity failed. With the variety of shapes and sizes of candles available today, it would be a shame not to decoupage them. Right now, decorated candles are very fashionable but they cost the earth. It's so much more rewarding to buy inexpensive plain candles and decorate them yourself for a fraction of the cost.

Almost anything can be used to decorate the candles: gift wrap, serviettes, transfers, dried flowers and so on. You can either paint the candle before decoupaging it or simply work directly onto the plain candle. Decoupaged candles are also easy and inexpensive gifts to make in a hurry. Sometimes candle medium has a tendency towards stickiness even when it is dry. A final coat of lacquer medium or water-based polyurethane varnish should sort out this problem.

RIGHT *Trying to glue paper cut-outs onto round candles would have been a nightmare but because the serviette is so fine and flexible, it took all of five minutes. The ivy works well on both types of candle because it can be either cut down or re-shaped.*

YOU WILL NEED

Paper/serviette of your choice
Modge Podge
Craft knife or scissors
Cutting mat
Candle
Methylated spirits or vinegar
Candle medium
Acrylic paint (optional)
Sponge applicator or flat soft
  synthetic brush
Kitchen wipe

1 Cut out the images you wish to use. If you're using gift wrap the images should be sealed with Modge Podge and left to dry before cutting. If using serviettes this is not necessary. Remember, only the top layer of the serviette is used.

2 Wipe the candle clean with either methylated spirits or vinegar and leave to dry. This is important otherwise the cut-outs won't stick properly.

3 If you want to paint the candle then now is the time to do it. Mix equal parts of medium with acrylic paint and either paint or sponge the mixture onto the candle. At least two to three coats are required and you should allow sufficient drying time after each coat. Leave to dry.

4 Using the sponge applicator, apply the candle medium to the back of the cut-out and place it in position on the candle. Press down firmly but carefully onto the cut-out with a damp kitchen wipe, working from one side to the other. If you're using a serviette, place the dry cut-out directly onto the candle and apply the candle medium over it, once again working from one side to the other. Make sure that all the bubbles are removed and edges are glued down properly. Leave to dry.

5 Apply a thin coat of candle medium to the entire candle. This is done for added protection to the cut-out as well as giving the candle a slight sheen.

HANDY HINTS

- As serviettes are easier to mould than paper, they are ideal if you want to decorate a candle by covering it completely. DO NOT try to cover thin candles though. They're not suitable for complete covering as the flame will ignite the paper or serviette. Use a candle of at least 5 cm in diameter because the wick burns down the centre and the flame will not reach the paper.
- Handle the candles carefully when they are wet otherwise you will leave fingerprints all over them.
- Instead of sealing the candle with medium, wax can be used to create a soft, romantic finish (see box on page 83).

Left An entire serviette was used to cover the circumference of the candles. This is a very quick way of decorating as no intricate cutting is involved. Only use thicker candles that will burn down in the centre otherwise the serviette will ignite.

SEALING WITH WAX

An interesting alternative to simply sealing the candle with medium is to use wax as a sealant. The effect is more muted and the images are buried in wax. This is especially effective when using dried flowers because it gives them added protection. The best wax to use for this purpose is candle-making wax which you should be able to find in most craft shops.

- Thoroughly clean the candle with methylated spirits, then glue on dried, pressed flowers with white wood-glue. Wipe away any excess glue around the flowers and leave to dry.
- Melt the wax (as you would chocolate) by using a double boiler or placing it in a heat resistant glass bowl over boiling water.
- Once the wax has melted completely, pour it into a container with a depth greater than the height of the candle. The amount of wax needed is about 75 per cent of the height of the candle. (Once the candle is placed inside the container with melted wax, the level of the wax rises to cover the candle.)
- Hold the candle by the wick (if this is too short, use tongs or pliers) and submerge the entire candle into the wax.

Lift it out, put the bottom end down onto a plate and allow to dry. If you notice any missed or uneven areas dip the candle a second time.

Soap

We have been asked on many occasions if soap could be decoupaged. The answer is, "Yes", but we couldn't quite work out why anybody would actually want to do this until we noticed these decoupaged soaps popping up all over the place in expensive gift and decorating shops – and selling extremely well. Not wanting to be left out, we started experimenting.

The first soap we made was sealed on the top with wax and was not a success. The reason for this is that one side of the soap would not lather at all and the underside had scratching ridges around it. So it was back to the drawing board to discover something else that would work. It didn't take us long to find out that the product that we were looking for was, in fact, candle or lacquer medium.

LEFT *These soaps are perfect quick-to-make gifts and stocking fillers. Serviettes, transfers and paper cutouts can be used. We don't recommend using pressed flowers or leaves in soap unless you never intend using the soap. They will come off as soon as the soap is first used for washing. If you do want to use these items for purely decorative soap, glue them on with white wood-glue and either leave as is or seal with wax.*

YOU WILL NEED

Serviettes or paper

Cutting mat

Craft knife or scissors

Modge Podge

Sponge applicator

Soap

Methylated spirits or vinegar

Candle or lacquer medium

Kitchen wipe

1 Cut out the images that you wish to use. We recommend serviettes, but if you want to use wrapping paper, the images should be sealed with Modge Podge and left to dry before cutting. If using serviettes this is not necessary. Again, only the top layer of the serviette is used.

2 Wipe the side of the soap that is going to be decorated with either methylated spirits or vinegar and leave to dry.

3 Using the sponge applicator, apply the medium to the back of the cut-out and place it in position on the soap. Press down firmly but carefully onto the cut-out with a damp kitchen wipe. If you are using a serviette, place the dry cut-out directly onto the soap and apply the candle medium over it, once again working from one side to the other. Ensure that all bubbles are removed and edges are glued down. Leave to dry.

4 Apply three to four coats of medium over the cut-out allowing drying time between coats.

HANDY HINTS

- Apply the picture to the underside of the soap so that the brand name doesn't show.
- Handmade soaps are attractive as a base as they offer different shapes and sizes.
- Handle the soaps carefully when they are wet otherwise the cut-outs will lift.
- If wrapping paper is used, more layers of medium are required for protection as the paper is thicker than serviettes.
- Transfers can also be used but only light coloured soaps are a suitable base otherwise the transfer will not be visible.
- Leave the soap to dry overnight (at least) before using it or wrapping it as a gift.

RIGHT *We decorated these lavender-scented soaps with paper cut-outs in order to stick to the lavender theme. When using paper cut-outs rather than serviettes, remember to apply the medium to the back of the cut-out as well as over it.*

Recycling

We decided to include this chapter after we were asked by our local school to give a lesson on decoupage. The class theme at the time was recycling which was a perfect way of getting around the problem of keeping costs down when teaching thirty children. We decided to decoupage on tin cans which the children made into pencil holders. The children loved the end result and we were amazed at how attractive these simple tins turned out.

This one course opened our eyes and once we started looking, we realized that almost anything can be recycled and decorated. We extended this beyond tin cans and boxes by delving into our storerooms and hauling out old junk that had been sitting there for years. These items took a little longer to complete as there is quite a bit of preparation involved. For this reason we are including tips on how to prepare various surfaces.

BELOW Old cardboard suitcases can be found in many junk shops (if you don't already have one floating around at home). This case was painted with a dark-blue acrylic paint and once the pictures were glued in place a heavy antique glaze was brushed over it to give it an aged look. Photocopies of family photographs can be used to turn it into a storage case for photo's.

RIGHT Give your toilet a facelift by decorating your wooden seat. Not only will you brighten up your home, it is sure to be a conversation piece for your guests. All traces of varnish need to be removed before you can begin. A heavy white colourwash was applied to the seat before the cut-outs were glued down. The images were cut from gift wrap and 4 coats of polyurethane varnish were applied to protect the surface.

Old wood

Old pieces with highly lacquered, polished or varnished surfaces all need a lot of preparation. This starts with wiping down the item with spirits or sugar soap to remove any wax or grease. When dry it should be sanded with coarse-grain sandpaper followed by another sanding with a finer grade paper. Only once the surface is smooth and free from anything sticky, shiny or flaking will you be able to work on it.

Painted wood

If you want to restore the wood back to its natural state you're going to have to use paint stripper. You will also have to strip it if it has many layers of paint that have chipped over the years – trying to sand through this lot will be a nightmare. Speak to your local hardware store for advice on the best product for the job and follow the instructions carefully. Remember to work in a well-ventilated room. If you prefer a distressed look (some people go to great lengths to achieve this) merely sand the painted surface until the desired look is achieved. If the surface has been painted with an oil-based product it needs a very good sanding before you can start decorating and may even need a coat of universal undercoat if you can't get rid of all traces of oil-based-paint or varnish.

ABOVE This galvanized steel 'plumber's tin' was spotted at the back of a hardware store. It needed a good scrub because it had been used to store all sorts of things. Once it was cleaned, primed and painted bright yellow, the images were glued into place. We used a computer printout for the letters which were painted green before being cut out and glued down. The tin was then antiqued to give it a softer, older look and finished off with 4 coats of oil-based varnish.

Old metal

The first thing you'll have to do is re-move any traces of rust by rubbing down rusty sections with fine steel wool. Follow this up by sanding the entire item lightly with 600-grit sandpaper. Apply a generous coat of a base-metal primer followed by a universal undercoat. Allow drying time in between coats. Now your metal is ready for decoupage.

Glass

Glass should be soaked in hot soapy water to remove any grime. If there is any paint on the glass this can be scraped off with a razor blade. The blade won't scratch the glass if you work carefully and it is held flat against the glass.

Finally, wipe the glass with spirits and dry thoroughly before begin-ning to decoupage.

LEFT *This portfolio holder was in such a bad state when we found it that it was immediately shoved away in a cupboard before we had the mental (and physical) energy to tackle it. All the metal was rusted and the case itself was covered in what can best be described as gunk! It needed to be scrubbed thoroughly with household cleaner first and then sanded down with coarse sandpaper. The metal bits had to be stripped and sanded down as well before any decoupaging could take place. Once all the preparation had been done, the paper was relaxed in water and then glued down using wallpaper paste. The case was then antiqued very slightly and finished off with 6 layers of polyurethane varnish.*

COVERING A CYLINDER

We have decided to take you step-by-step and show you how to cover a curved object completely with paper. Once we discovered this easy method of applying paper to a curved surface we laughed at the hours we'd spent previously struggling with creases and wrinkles.

1 Paint the cylinder with at least two coats of base paint to prevent any images on the cylinder from showing through the wrapping paper. Apply one coat of Modge Podge. Allow to dry. Apply one coat of Modge Podge to the printed side of the paper you've selected. Leave to dry.

2 Cut the paper to approximately the correct size by wrapping it around the cylinder to see how much you'll need. Ensure that you cut the vertical sides straight to achieve a neat finish. Cut the bottom edge of the paper slightly longer than the cylinder. It will be trimmed later.

3 Relax the paper by soaking it in a bowl of warm water until the paper stops curling. Don't leave it in longer than this otherwise the paper could be damaged. While the paper is soaking apply an even coat of white wood-glue to the cylinder.

4 Remove the paper from the water and gently shake off excess water. Start applying the paper to the tube working slowly around the cylinder.

YOU WILL NEED
A cylinder (Pringles tins are ideal)
Broken-white PVA base coat
Modge Podge
Sponge applicator
Wrapping paper
Craft knife
White wood-glue
Kitchen wipe

Smooth out any bubbles and wrinkles as you go along. You will find that the paper doesn't 'fight' back as the fibres have been relaxed.

5 Balance the cylinder on a jar in order to prevent the overhanging paper from being damaged. Leave to dry. Trim away excess paper with a craft knife and seal with three to four coats of water-based varnish.

HANDY HINTS

- You can also cover the tube in fabric, glued on with white wood-glue (follow the instructions on page 78).
- The tube can be painted with three to four coats of acrylic paint and cut-outs can be used to decoupage it further rather than making use of complete covering only.
- The 'relaxing' technique can be used with any paper images (including cut-outs) that are going to be glued onto a curved surface, for example a bowl or an ostrich egg.

COVERING A TEA BOX

These recycled tea boxes not only make attractive gift presentation boxes but are also useful as storage containers. They are quick and easy to make and only one or two coats of varnish are required to complete your project.

YOU WILL NEED
Cardboard tea box
Craft knife
Cutting mat
Wrapping paper
Modge Podge
Sponge applicator
White wood-glue
Water-based varnish
Wrapping paper
Rubber roller
Kitchen wipe

1 Carefully separate the glued inner flaps of the box in order to flatten the box. It should come apart easily but, if not, a craft knife slid into the joins will do the trick.

2 Apply one coat of Modge Podge to the wrapping paper. Once it is dry, cut two pieces large enough to cover both sides of the cardboard. Apply one coat of Modge Podge to each side of the cardboard, allowing drying time in between.

3 Apply watered-down white wood-glue (3 parts glue to 1 part water) to one side of the cardboard. Place one piece of paper over the cardboard and, using a roller and a damp kitchen wipe to protect the paper, start gluing down by rolling from the top corner to the bottom corner. Roll down firmly and check your work as you go along to avoid creases and folds. Remove the covered cardboard from the surface that you are working on and allow to dry.

4 Turn the cardboard over and, using a craft knife, trim away all excess paper. Repeat steps three and four on the other side of the cardboard, using the other piece of paper.

HANDY HINTS

- Before gluing ensure that the wrapping paper you are using will be facing the right way up once the box has been reconstructed.
- This technique is only suitable for fairly thin cardboard because if it is too thick the wrapping paper will tear when you reconstruct the box.
- When gluing make sure that you don't glue the cardboard to the surface that you are working on, it can easily happen.

- If you have damaged the paper during gluing and reconstructing, remember coloured pencils will cover a lot of mistakes. Remedy these before you apply the first coat of varnish.
- Using different prints on the inside and the outside gives a tea box and interesting appearance. You can also use a patterned paper on one side and a matching plain paper on the other side.
- Recycle other boxes, such as a whisky box, in the same way.

5 Reconstruct the box and glue into position using white wood-glue. Clothes pegs can be used to clamp the sides together until they have dried. Apply one to two coats of varnish to the entire box, leaving drying time in between coats.

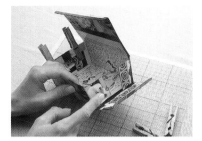

BELOW *The tea-cup images on this paper seemed perfect for covering tea boxes. Both boxes were covered inside with paper that complimented the design used on the outside. If you use your imagination, these pretty boxes could be used for tea bags, as gift presentation boxes or storing all those bits and pieces lying around in your kitchen.*

Papier-mâché

When we were discussing ideas for the recycled section, papier-mâché immediately came to mind. It was supposed to be a small part of the section on recycling but when we saw what could be done, it turned into a section of its own.

Like most people, the only experience we'd ever had of papier-mâché was as children layering sticky pieces of newspaper over a balloon and painting the finished wobbly bowl with some gaudy designs that only a mother could love. Traditionally papier-mâché has been bold and colourful and there is definitely a place for that but we also wanted to try to present it in a more subtle and stylish way. We experimented with different papers and glues (because there are various ways to approach this craft) and eventually hit upon the technique best suited for our needs.

Despite the French name, papier-mâché actually originated in China. The French name simply means 'chewed paper' which makes us wonder how exactly the French prepared their paper! We don't suggest you sit in front of the TV chewing the daily newspaper in preparation for your project because we've found a much easier way.

Be warned: papier-mâché is messy, you'll get glue all over your hands and work surface, you won't be able to answer the phone while working with it and because it's so messy you'll definitely have offers of help from the kids. Let them help or give them their own project to do.

LEFT *This set was made using three different methods for the various items. The cup was a ready- made paper pulp one bought at a nursery, the bowl was made from tissue paper rather than newspaper (which gives it a more delicate look) and the box was made by making up a cardboard box first and then covering it with newspaper. All the items were covered with torn pieces of handmade paper using the papier-mâché method (two layers were needed) and sealed with three layers of water-based polyurethane varnish.*

YOU WILL NEED

Newspaper

White wood-glue

Mould with smooth sides

Petroleum jelly

Paint brush

Sponge applicator

300-grit sandpaper

Broken-white PVA base coat

400-grit sandpaper

Water-based varnish

1 Tear the newspaper into narrow strips, about 2 cm wide and 10 cm long (unless the mould is much smaller in which case the strips will be shorter). Mix the glue with an equal amount of water in a small bowl.

2 Smear petroleum jelly over the mould to prevent the papier-mâché from sticking when dry. You can use the outside or the inside of the mould. If the mould has a lip, however, you'll find that it's a lot easier to remove the mould on completion if you work on the inside surface.

3 Dampen the strips (one at a time) with glue either by using a paint brush or by dipping them into the glue. If you've decided to cover the outside surface then turn the mould upside down and, starting at the top, work around and down the mould, overlapping the strips slightly until it is evenly covered. If you are working inside the mould then you should work from the bottom upwards.

4 Next lay down dry strips of paper, but in order to prepare for this, you'll first need to paint a layer of glue over the entire surface on which you've been working. The dry strips should be applied horizontally to give the article added strength. Lay the first strip into position and paint over it with glue. Continue in this fashion until the entire surface has been covered, pushing out any air bubbles and excess glue as you go along.

5 Continue working at these steps until you have built up at least eight layers of paper. More layers will be necessary for larger items. If you find that the bottom of the bowl is becoming much thicker than the rest, omit one or two layers in that area (but not the last one otherwise the finished item will be too uneven).

6 Leave to dry in a warm place. Drying can take anything between 24 hours and a week, depending on the temperature and number of layers. Remember, just because the outer layer is dry that doesn't mean it's dry all the way through. Once dry, the papier-mâché should slide easily off the mould if you gently run a knife between the mould and newspaper. If the knife comes out with bits of damp paper on it, the papier-mâché is not dry and needs to be left longer.

ABOVE *A metal baking tin was used as a mould for the papier-mâché bowl. The cup was made by Natasha, our 12-year-old assistant who wanted to get in on the act and used one of her plastic drinking cups as a mould. The images were cut from gift wrap and decoupaged in the usual way.*

7 Once you have freed the papier-mâché, patch up any damaged areas with extra paper if necessary. You can even add an extra layer if you need to. Once dry, trim any uneven edges with a pair of scissors.

Sand the entire bowl, inside and out, with 300-grit sandpaper to smooth out rough edges.

Extra strips of newspaper can be wrapped and glued over the rim of the papier mache bowl once it has been removed from the mould . This gives the edges a smoother look and also prevents the layers from separating if they haven't been glued firmly enough. Leave to dry.

8 Apply one coat of PVA to the entire bowl. Once dry, sand the bowl again, this time with 400-grit sandpaper. Your bowl is now ready to be decoupaged.

9 Paint and decorate the bowl as you would any other raw decoupage blank. Multiple layers of varnish may be used to 'bury' the print or simply apply four to six layers of water-based varnish to finish it off.

HANDY HINTS

- You may prefer to allow each layer to dry before applying the next, this is entirely up to you.
- If the papier-mâché seems too flimsy, add another couple of layers of newspaper, either to the outside or inside.
- Papier-mâché is fairly sturdy, but it is mainly decorative. It would be fine to hold dry items, like nuts for example, but forget about using it as a fruit bowl. The moisture from the fruit would eventually ruin it.
- For a really delicate look, use tissue paper to make the bowl, you could even place glitter or dried petals between the layers, making it unnecessary to decoupage the bowl afterwards.
- As papier-mâché is never completely smooth, images seem to bury a lot quicker that on traditional flat surfaces.
- For a smoother finish on papier-mâché, mix wood filler with water and paint it over the item before preparing it for decoupage. Leave to dry and sand lightly with 400-grit sandpaper.

Colourwashed wood

This section was going to be decoupage on natural wood but experience has shown us that decoupaging straight onto most woods invariably looks a little too stark and the wood can often overpower the image (or sometimes the other way around). So, at the last minute, we decided to change the section to decoupaging on wood that has been colourwashed (often mistakenly referred to as 'liming'). We prefer this look ourselves as it gives the finished article far more subtlety. Also, it's a very popular finish and we're constantly being asked how to do it.

The whole point of colourwashing is to change the basic colour of the wood while still allowing the attractive grain to show through. By 'knocking the wood back' a little with a wash a more subtle, pastel background is created which lends itself more readily to a pleasing final effect. Bear in mind though that this finish should really be done on raw wood. In other words, the same effect cannot be achieved by colourwashing over varnished or oiled wood. If you have something lying around that you wish to decoupage in this way but it's covered in varnish, oil or lacquer, it will have to be cleaned and sanded thoroughly before you can begin working.

RIGHT *This look is not really colourwashed wood; it is more of a distressed look. Three coats of white wash (without scumble glaze) were applied to the writing box. Once dry the box was sanded quite heavily, particularly around the edges where natural wear would take place. We wanted to move away from the nautical look normally associated with this type of finish and the Michelangelo image was a perfect way of doing this because it was also rather worn-looking.*

Raw wooden blank
Sponge applicator
Modge Podge
400-grit sandpaper
White acrylic paint
Acrylic scumble glaze
2 small paint brushes

BELOW *The serviette from which we cut the feather and quills for these items was probably the most unexciting serviette that we had ever seen. However, once the images were cut away from their dull, dark background and put onto a lighter one, they really came to life. We wanted to create an 'African feel' without using the traditional dark colours usually associated with this look.*

1 Apply one coat of Modge Podge to the entire item. Allow to dry and sand with 400-grit sandpaper. Apply a second coat of Modge Podge. The second coat seals the wood and prevents it from becoming rough or 'hairy' when you apply the wash.

2 Make up a wash by mixing together white paint, scumble glaze and water. The ratio is: 1 part paint, 1 part scumble glaze and 2 parts water. Make sure that you have everything ready for the next step (including the 2 brushes) because it has to be done quickly.

3 Working quickly, brush on the wash following the grain of the wood, working from one side of the item to the other in one movement. If the finish looks too streaky brush over it with a dry brush in order to blend

it in (once again working with the grain). Finish one side before moving onto the next because the wash dries fairly quickly and it's difficult to rectify mistakes once the wash has dried. When the wash has dried and you're satisfied with the effect, apply a coat of Modge Podge to the entire painted area and allow to dry

4 Decoupage as you would any other painted item. Seal with four to six coats of varnish to complete.

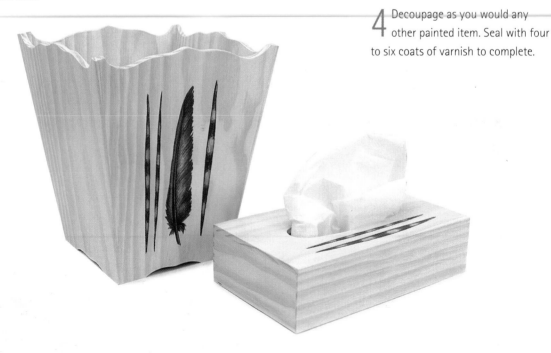

HANDY HINTS

- If the wash is too subtle for your taste, wait for it to dry and apply a second coat.
- Should the finish be a complete disaster, simply wipe it off with soap and water, leave to dry completely and redo.
- Be careful not to touch the wash while it is still wet otherwise you will leave fingerprints.
- This finish is not exclusively for decoupage items – it can be applied to furniture as well. You would need to increase the ratio of scumble glaze for larger items in order to give yourself more time to 'work' the paint; the item should then be sealed with an oil-based varnish to give it added protection.
- You don't have to stick to white when applying a wash – any colour can be used.
- If you would still like to experiment for yourself with various natural woods follow step 1 for basic preparation of your surface and skip steps 2 and 3.

BELOW These inexpensive pine packaging boxes were picked up from a florist's shop and transformed into planters using a simple colourwash. The images were cut from gift wrap and a polyurethane varnish was used to seal the planters in order to give them the extra protection needed to withstand a certain amount of water.

Nature

It's all very well decoupaging with pictures of feathers and shells for instance, but often nothing beats the real thing. A walk on a beach or even through your own garden will yield many treasures. In our quest for guinea fowl feathers we went traipsing through the bush around Knysna, following the sounds of some pretty but frustratingly-elusive and noisy birds. We eventually returned triumphantly with the grand total of two feathers and can assure you that not a single bird was harmed in the process! Luckily we managed to source a few elsewhere which was just as well because we'd decided that our alternative career as big-game hunters was over after a spider the size of a Podge bottle was spotted relaxing on Tracy's head and Deborah got icky mud all over her new boots. The bush is all very well but you can't get a decent cappuccino there.

Flowers are a little easier to find (well, they don't keep running away for a start) and even easier to press. We even bought a special flower-press for this purpose, only to find out that it worked no better than placing the flowers between the pages of a heavy book and pressing them that way. Some plants work better than others so you'll have to experiment but avoid any 'rubbery' types as they really don't press well. We've chosen to demonstrate on a wooden box but this technique can also be used on galvanized steel, candles and unglazed pottery (refer to the relevant chapters for preparation).

LEFT *A plain frame and inexpensive lamp were transformed by the use of autumn leaves. The lampshade is galvanized steel and the base a pine one that was streaked with various shades of red and brown to give the impression of dark wood. It was easier to work with the leaves before they were completely dry because they had to be moulded. Once the leaves had been glued into place on the frame (and this took time and patience) they were left to dry and the excess bits trimmed away later. Both items were finished off with 6 coats of oil-based varnish for added protection.*

YOU WILL NEED
Wooden decoupage blank
Broken-white PVA paint
Wood filler
400-grit sandpaper
Acrylic craft paint
Modge Podge
Foam applicator
Pressed flower
White wood-glue
Varnish

BELOW *The corrugated envelopes and bag were purchased at our local hardware store and decorated using handmade paper and various dried flowers and leaves. Both the dried flowers and paper were glued down using white wood-glue to ensure firm adhesion. Don't try to use a roller to glue the paper on otherwise you will flatten the ridges in the cardboard. These make perfect gift presentation boxes.*

1 Apply a base coat of broken-white PVA to the blank and leave to dry. Fill any holes or blemishes and sand with 400-grit sandpaper when dry. Paint it with the desired colour (at least four coats). Apply one coat of Modge Podge and leave to dry.

2 Decide where you would like to place the flower. Apply a gener-

ous amount of glue to the area where the flower is to be placed. Press the flower into position on top of the glue. It may be necessary to continue pressing down on the flower until it adheres to the surface.

3 Clean away all excess glue from around the flower and if any sections have lifted, re-glue and clean around them again. Allow to dry.

4 Apply at least six coats of varnish of your choice to the entire object, allowing sufficient drying time between coats.

HANDY HINTS

- When gluing down feathers, brush the feathers into shape with a toothbrush.
- If a stalk or flower seems too thick, it can be trimmed down with a craft knife.
- Autumn leaves dry very quickly. We've found that they are best used four days after pressing, or they become too brittle.

- Use your imagination – virtually anything can be used. Pebbles, driftwood, shells and pods also look good. Any of these items combined with handmade paper as a background looks very effective.
- Work very carefully when using pressed flowers; always bear in mind that they are delicate.

RESIN

Resin can be used to complete your item. We've found that the best way to do this (especially with shells and multi-leafed plants) is by pouring two layers of resin, allowing drying time between each pouring. The reason for a 'double-pouring' is that you'll probably get lots of bubbles which need to be pricked. This will take time and it's quite possible that you'll be left with dents in the resin which can be corrected with a second pouring. Leave the first layer to dry for 48 hours. Sand with 400-grit sandpaper and dust off before pouring a second layer.

BELOW The lavender-coloured paint used for the tray complimented the colour of the dry lavender flowers. It is also better to use a darker background when pouring a thick layer of resin because of the 'yellowing' effect of the resin. The dried lavender flowers were glued down and then the whole plant pot antiqued with a raw-umber glaze to give it a more aged look. The same glaze was used over the green sections of the tray to marry the two items together.

Iron-on transfers

You now know how to put serviettes onto fabric but what happens if you have a picture that you'd like to transfer onto a cushion in order to match it to the wastepaper basket that you made last week? Iron-on transfers are the answer. You'll be able to create beautiful scatter cushions for a fraction of the price that you'd pay in an interior decorating shop. You are not limited to cushions either: how about copying your children's artwork onto transfer paper and making them placemats? Transfers placed on loose chair covers and the edges of curtains also look good.

Before you rush out, buy transfers from your local hardware store and start ironing them onto cushions – stop! Specific fabric iron-on transfer paper must be used. You can either buy this paper from good computer stationers or from photocopy shops. Once you've decided on the image that you want to transfer, it needs to be photocopied onto the transfer paper. Even though it is cheaper to make these cushions yourself rather than buy ready-made ones, the transfer paper is obviously more expensive than plain bond paper. Therefore it is advisable to copy as many images onto one sheet as possible. Cut out the paper images before taking them to be photocopied onto transfer paper: that way they can be placed close together. The drawback of this technique is that you have only one chance to get it right. It isn't difficult but we suggest that you read through all the instructions before starting your project.

RIGHT *These exquisite images were taken from gift wrap and photocopied to make transfers. As the cushions are different sizes we were able to reduce and enlarge the images to suit the size of the cushions. The original borders of the pictures had straight lines but we decided to reshape them to soften them.*

YOU WILL NEED
Transfer
Craft knife or scissors
Fabric
Cutting mat
Iron

1 Cut out the images that you wish to use from the transfer and cut them out. A pair of scissors or a craft knife will do the trick.

2 Iron the fabric before beginning to work on it.

3 Decide where the image is to be placed. It may be necessary to use a ruler in order to line it up straight. Don't use a fabric marker otherwise you could end up ironing in the mark permanently if the transfer goes over it. Turn your iron on to a cotton setting (no steam) and leave to heat up.

4 Once the transfer is in position (with the image facing down-wards) you can begin ironing over the backing paper. Iron very firmly and slowly, keeping the iron moving in order to avoid burning the backing

paper. The backing paper should start lifting at the corners after about 10 to 15 seconds. Once it does you can begin peeling the paper off. If it sticks, then stop and apply more heat to that area and resume peeling.

5 Leave it to cool completely for about 20 minutes and then iron again on the reverse side of the fabric. This heat-seals it for washing.

LEFT There were supposed to be two cushions here but it was our first attempt and we messed up the first one! We didn't apply enough heat to the transfer (and also removed it too quickly); consequently the image came out very faded. It actually didn't look too bad until we made the second one, put them next to each other and then noticed the difference in colour intensity.

HANDY HINTS

- We strongly recommend that you use the transfer off-cuts (even if they have no picture or colour) to practise with in order to get the technique right. It doesn't take long to perfect and at least you won't end up making costly mistakes.
- As the image will be reversed once it is ironed on, remember to ask for it to be reversed when photocopying it. This is especially important when you are transferring writing.
- Do not use the iron on its steam setting.
- Use fabrics in lighter colours, otherwise the transfer will disappear into the background.
- Do not wash the fabric for at least 24 hours after applying the transfer to give it time to set.
- Don't wash transfer-decorated fabric with strong washing powders or bleach and don't tumble dry or dry clean them.
- Iron transfer-decorated items on the reverse side of the fabric and not directly onto the transferred image.

RIGHT *Once the transfer had been made the image was cut away from the background before being applied to the neck-pillow cover. As the image contained wording, it had to be photocopied in reverse to avoid the words appearing back to front. The remaining images left on the print were used to decorate lavender bags.*